CAREERS
IN THE
MILITARY

Robert Rafferty

☆☆☆☆☆☆☆☆☆☆☆☆☆☆☆☆☆☆☆☆☆☆☆☆☆☆☆☆☆☆☆☆

CAREERS IN THE MILITARY

☆☆☆☆☆☆☆☆☆☆☆☆☆☆☆☆☆☆☆☆☆☆☆☆☆☆☆☆☆☆☆☆

Good Training for Civilian Life

ELSEVIER/NELSON BOOKS
New York

Library of Congress Cataloging in Publication Data

Rafferty, Robert.
  Careers in the military.

  Bibliography: p.
  Includes index.
  1. United States—Armed Forces—Vocational guidance.   I. Title.
UB147.R33 1980   355'.0023'73   80-11390
ISBN 0-525-66668-0

Published in the United States by Elsevier/Nelson Books, a division of Elsevier-Dutton Publishing Company, Inc., New York. Published simultaneously in Don Mills, Ontario, by Nelson/Canada.

10 9 8 7 6 5 4 3 2 1

Contents

CAREERS
IN THE
MILITARY

Author's Note

Our armed forces are in the process of constant change. Therefore, because of the time involved in writing and publishing any book, some of the information in this one will probably have changed by the time you read it. This is particularly true of the details on pay, enlistment options, educational programs, and job qualifications. To get the most up-to-date information you should check with the recruiting offices of the various services.

Despite this, the thrust of this book is still valid and will not become outdated. You *can* use the military to start a lifelong civilian career.

Another point to note is that even though each of the five services is different in philosophy, mission, and life-style, there are many areas of similarity and even duplication when it comes to what they have to offer you. If I gave all the details about each service on each subject there would be a great deal of repetition, and this compact book would grow as large as an unabridged dictionary.

To avoid that, I've pulled out the general information that loosely applies to all the services and then illustrated each point with examples from one or more services. If this technique seems to weigh heavily toward one service it is unintentional. I have tried to spread the coverage evenly among all five. If any service got the short end of the stick it is probably the Coast Guard, but that's only because it is such a small service and also because it is the only one not under the Department of Defense. This unique position made it inappropriate to use as an example in many cases. But that in no way lessens the attractiveness of the Coast Guard if you find it fills your needs.

CHAPTER ONE

A Choice Worth Considering

"What are you going to be when you grow up?"

How many times have you been asked that question? Well, *now* it's getting to the time when you'll have to come up with an answer. You are either at or reaching the age of choice—the age when you can decide what you will be now that you *are* grown up.

If you are the average young person you have little real knowledge of the wide world of work. Sure, you've worked part-time in a fast-food place or a store and had summer jobs, but those jobs just earned you pocket money. Now you are leaving the protected world of the classroom and the sheltered world of home and stepping into the highly competitive world of work in which you'll have to survive for the rest of your life.

What do you know about the world of work? Are you aware of the incredible range of career alternatives that are available to you? Are you prepared to step into it and go after a worthwhile career? Or are you, like most young people, looking forward to finding your place in the world but still unsure and a little scared?

You are entering a vast labor pool—a pool in which you'll have to sink or swim on your own merits. What are your prospects? Do you have a skill some employer will be willing to pay for? What's the job market like in your area, and how do you fit into it? And if you do find a job you like, what pay and fringe benefits can you expect at the start? At the end of the first year? And after five years or more on the job?

These questions are the type you should be asking yourself—and trying to answer honestly. And you should ask them now while you have time and before you're pressured into taking a job you don't really want.

EXPERIENCE—THE "CATCH 22"

When you start job hunting, one of the first questions employers will ask is, "What experience do you have?" If you're just out of high school you won't have much to offer. As a result, if you are hired, all you can expect is the lowest-paying job, and then you'll be the first one laid off if times get tough.

How do you get the experience the boss wants? Simple—you get it by working. And this brings on the "Catch 22," because you can only get a good job if you have experience, but you can't get experience without a job.

According to the Department of Labor, if you want to succeed in the 1980's you had better start learning a technical specialty now. Because of the tremendous surge in technological know-how, it is expected that between 1980 and 1990 four out of five jobs will require technical rather than academic training.

Technical training is expensive, and few companies offer it to new employees. If you want it, the odds are you'll have to go to night school while on the job and pay for your own advancement.

You should also realize that it is tough even to get a foot in the door of some civilian trades. In addition, they are highly competitive and require long years in apprenticeship programs before you can expect to earn good pay.

So there's your problem: you need both technical training and experience if you want to get a good career job.

A PRACTICAL SOLUTION

Knowing this, how would you like to open the "Help Wanted" section of your newspaper and read the following ad:

HELP WANTED—NO EXPERIENCE NECESSARY!

Hard but challenging jobs leading to careers. Long hours, frequent moves, some danger, but employer offers: early responsibility and unlimited opportunity for advancement, extensive education in the field of your choice if you are qualified, one month's vacation a year, many paid holidays, free medical and dental care, almost unlimited sick leave, free or low-cost recreational facilities, chance for world-wide travel. Starting pay over $400 a month, with guaranteed raise after six months, free housing or tax-free housing allowance, free meals or tax-free meal allowance. Also extra pay for special skills or dangerous assignments, cost-of-living raises, and many other benefits. Outstanding retirement benefits. Open to all males and females in good health aged 17 and up. High-school diploma preferred.

Since you know the title of this book, it's no secret that this ad is for an enlistment in one of our five armed services: Air Force, Army, Coast Guard, Marines, and Navy. It's an offer to join the more than 2 million men and women already holding full-time jobs in uniform.

Enlisting in the armed forces is just about the only way you can get both technical training and job experience and get paid while you're doing it.

The military will take you in as a raw, unskilled recruit and spend a fortune training you so you can get ahead both in the service and out. Even if you don't especially care for the idea of a career in the military—and that's a decision you shouldn't make until you've tried it—you can still take advantage of what the military has to offer you as one of the best training grounds for any civilian skill. You'll get both classroom and on-the-job training, and unlike civilian schooling, the world of school and the world of work are just extensions of each other in the military. You're trained to do a particular job and then you do it.

Do the armed forces want you?

You bet they do! Because of turnover, it takes about a thousand volunteers a day to keep the five services at full strength.

What jobs are available?

Almost anything you'd like. For example, the Army alone lists over 400 different military occupational specialties (read that "jobs") in 36 career fields, and you can get professional training in all of them. Of course, all those jobs aren't open to new recruits. Many require advanced training and experience. But more than half are listed as "entry-level" jobs; that is, they are the first, or entry, jobs in the career field. From them you go up the ladder.

The military will test you and train you in the career field in which you show the greatest aptitude and where you are most likely to succeed. They will even enter into a written contract with you before you enlist, guaranteeing that you'll get the specific training for which you are qualified.

GO IN WITH YOUR EYES WIDE OPEN

You must understand right from the start, however, that what you're getting into is not just another job. First of all, the military will make a firm commitment to train you, but you in turn must sign up for a definite number of years of duty, and the military will hold you to that.

Next, as mentioned in the help-wanted ad, military life can be demanding, and may often require personal sacrifice. You may have to shoulder heavy responsibilities, even the awesome responsibility of risking your own life or the lives of others. You'll need both physical and emotional stamina, because at times you'll come under great stress and have to prove yourself to both the world and to yourself.

And, as we all know, the military demands discipline. But don't get that wrong. They are not trying to turn you into a machine. Don't look for chances to be an individual in basic training or even during your first year on the job, but after you've proved yourself you'll find that individual thinking is highly prized and has a large place in the military. That's what distinguishes our military men from those in the military machines behind the Iron and Bamboo curtains.

So if you want a life that's never going to be demanding of your time, energy, or abilities, you'd best look elsewhere. This book is not for you.

DON'T LET THIS TURN YOU OFF

What I just said is not intended to discourage you or turn you off to the good things in the military. It is only to make certain you have a clear view of military life as it is in reality, not as seen in the recruiting films or through the recruiter's rose-colored glasses.

You've probably heard a thousand stories about the unpopular side of military life—the horror stories about basic training, hurry-up-and-wait, KP, getting scalped at the barber's, uniform regulations, restrictions on when and where you can go, stupid noncommissioned officers (NCO's) and bullheaded officers, and the dreary discipline of doing everything by the numbers.

There used to be truth in all those tales—and in an organization of 2 million people some of the stories are still bound to be true—but since the draft ended in 1973 the military has undergone significant changes, and most of them were for the better. Basic training is still rough, but not the hell it used to be, not even in the Marines. A lot of what the troops called "Mickey Mouse"—nitpicking annoyances—is gone. Not all of it, but most of it. The old-time barracks you saw so often in old war movies have mostly been replaced by buildings that resemble college dorms. In some the servicemen have double rooms with air conditioning, carpets, draperies, and the freedom to decorate. Officially they aren't even called barracks anymore; they're "living quarters."

It's still a long way from heaven, but then what job is heaven?

You'll be treated like an adult and given security in your job and a guaranteed wage, but you'll be expected to give a lot in return. Although you'll routinely have plenty of free time, when the chips are down and your service is doing its thing, it's a total-commitment job, and you'll be expected to be there working nonstop, without extra pay, because that's the name of the game in the military.

One other thing you should know right at the start: if you don't like going to school, don't enlist to get out of it.

First of all, the services all want high-school graduates. The experiences they have had trying to train high-school dropouts hasn't been good.

Second, if you want to get ahead you have to be ready, willing, and eager either to go to school or study correspondence courses on your own. The military knows that knowledge is power. They all need highly trained professionals. They don't have the time or the money to put up with a man or woman who can't or won't learn.

In fact, if you do join up, you'll find your buddies are probably a lot smarter than you expected. Although there will always be a military job for someone willing to work hard but without the ability to learn a technical skill, the military has become more and more involved with complex machinery and equipment, and the people who use and maintain these sophisticated items can't be dopes. Even in the Army, which is still basically a mud-slugging, ground-pounding organization, two out of three soldiers have at *least* a high-school education. And the educational level has been rising steadily.

If you realize that there are some unpleasant things about military life—things the recruiters rarely mention—and enlist with a clear view of the good and the bad points, you'll have a better chance of being happy in your decision.

I said "the good and the bad points," but so far most of what has been covered are the bad points. If you haven't been scared off, you'll find the rest of this book pretty much devoted to the good points. But it views them realistically: no candy-coating. When you finish reading this, you'll probably conclude that the military offers a challenging and satisfying life-style that will make up for the few hardships many times over. Studies have shown that overall job satisfaction is high in the military and that career personnel are happy in their choice.

Whether or not it's for you, only you can decide.

IS THERE A PLACE FOR WOMEN?

Women are taking an increasingly larger role in the military every year. The services are actively working to increase the number of women from about five out of every hundred to at least seven out of a hundred by the early 1980's. There are good reasons for this, as you'll see when you read the chapter on women in the service, but what it means statistically is that there will soon be over 150,000 women in uniform.

Not too long ago a woman in the military was either a nurse or a secretary or a clerk. Now women are in all fields except actual combat—and even that barrier is being challenged. In all the services women are working as everything from aircraft mechanics to pilots, truck drivers to 'dozer operators, telephone linemen to members of parachute demonstration teams. Of the four hundred specialties available in the Army, only sixteen combat jobs are not open to women.

Admittedly, some of this is a publicity front, but as more and more women prove they can do the jobs, the equality is becoming more and more real. Overall, you'll probably find that equality is closer to the ideal in the services than in most large civilian organizations.

HOW THIS BOOK CAN HELP YOU

Making a career decision is never easy and one of the most difficult things about it is getting accurate information on which to base your choice. The purpose of this book is to give you that accurate information in a form you can understand, leaving out all the buzzwords and bureaucratic cover-ups.

This book is designed to give such information to the young man or woman thinking of going into the service for the first time.

It is not designed to sell you on a career in the military, but merely to introduce you to what you might get from a few years in uniform. Whether you get out at the end of your first tour of duty and use your training and experience in the civilian job market or stay in and go on to a military career is up to you.

I could fill an encyclopedia with details of all the ways to enlist, of all the jobs available, of how to get into one of the academies or career programs, and of a thousand other aspects, but at this stage in your decision making all that would be useless to you. What you need to know is what the various services offer to you on your first tour of duty as an enlisted man (or woman) or officer. Although the book mentions benefits and programs that you can only get at after you've been in the service for a time, the largest part is devoted to what you need to know to take the first steps and get through the first few months. Once you are in the service you'll have plenty of time and opportunity to find out about the other things that will advance your career or improve your life-style.

So much for an introduction. Now let's get on with it!

CHAPTER TWO

The Paycheck with the Fringe on Top

One of the first things most people ask about a job is, "How much does it pay?"

Before World War II there was a song about military pay that said a soldier received "twenty-one dollars a day—once a month." Military pay has come a long way from $21 a month.

All military pay has gone up steadily, both to keep military salaries as close as possible to salaries for equivalent civilian jobs, and to keep up with the cost of living. For example, in 1967 a recruit earned about $100 a month base pay; now it is about $450 a month. In that same year the lowest-grade officer, a second lieutenant in the Air Force, Army, or Marines, or an ensign in the Coast

Guard or Navy, earned $321 a month base pay; now it's well over $800.

"BASE PAY"—WHAT DOES IT MEAN?

The pay you earn is divided into several parts, some taxable and some nontaxable. Your basic salary is called "base pay"; it's taxable. Your base pay is your starting point. To this may be added a number of allowances and some extra pay, which all add up to your total pay. Your total pay depends on your particular situation: your job, dependents, location, and a few other things.

When you talk about pay you must also talk about rank. The services all have different titles for the various ranks or grades. For example, the day you join the Air Force you become an airman basic; in the Coast Guard and Navy you're a seaman recruit; the Army calls you a recruit; and the Marines give you the title of private. But when it comes to pay you are listed as enlisted grade 1, or an E-1, in every service, and your base pay will be exactly the same in every service. The E-grades are enlisted pay grades. For officers, as you can easily guess, it's an O-grade. That second lieutenant or ensign mentioned above is in grade 0-1.

A partial list of comparative grades and titles is included in this chapter. A full list appears in Appendix A.

Military pay isn't just based on rank, but also on years of service. That means you not only get a pay raise every time you earn a promotion, but also every time you reach a certain number of years' service—sort of an anniversary present. When you're first starting out, pay jumps come automatically after two, three, and four years of service. After that they normally come every two years.

So it's possible to have several pay raises in one year. Let's see how that might work. You start off as an E-1 with a base pay of $448 a month. Either right after basic training, or at the latest within six months after you enlist, you'll be promoted to E-2 and get raised to $500. Then, if you work hard it's possible to make E-3 early in your second year and that would mean a jump to $519. Once you complete two years of service that goes up to $548, an increase of over $100 a month in just two years.

In addition, there is usually an automatic cost-of-living increase every year; most recent ones have been 5 to 7 percent. Using 7 percent as an example, your pay as an E-3 would more likely be close to $586.

And that's just base pay. We haven't looked at allowances and other pay yet.

(The pay information used in this book is correct at the time of publication, but because of the annual cost-of-living increases it is probably already out of date. For your planning you can use these figures as the *least* you'll get because there has not been a pay cutback since before World War II. You can get the exact pay scale from the recruiters.)

Here is an extract of the pay grades and ranks you'll be interested in initially either as an enlisted recruit or a new officer. A complete pay scale is listed in Appendix B.

Note that the increases stop in each pay grade after so many years of service. In fact, E-1 and E-2 never do get a raise because there'd be something wrong with you and your career if you are still in either of those grades after

Pay Grade	Title	Cumulative Years of Service			
		Under 2	Over 2	Over 3	Over 4
E-1	AF: Airman Basic Army: Recruit CG/Navy: Seaman Recruit Marines: Private	$448	—	—	—
E-2	AF: Airman Army: Private CG/Navy: Seaman Apprentice Marines: Private First Class	$500	—	—	—
E-3	AF: Airman First Class Army: Private First Class CG/Navy: Seaman Marines: Lance Corporal	$519	$548	$570	$592
O-1	AF/Army/Marines: Second Lieutenant CG/Navy: Ensign	$827	$861	$1041	—
O-2	AF/Army/Marines: First Lieutenant CG/Navy: Lieutenant Junior Grade	$953	$1041	$1250	$1293

two years. This is the military's way of giving you an incentive to work your way up. It's also a warning that if you don't go up the ladder you'll be getting out.

Just as in civilian life, you'll have deductions taken out of your pay for income tax and social security. But next we'll look at some allowances that are tax-free.

TAX-FREE ALLOWANCES

If you are not provided government living quarters you'll be paid quarters allowance as follows:

Pay grade	If you're single	If you're married or have a legal dependent
E-1	$92	$160
E-2	$97	$160
E-3	$110	$160
O-1	$168	$219
O-2	$215	$272

It's not very likely that the circumstances would be such that you wouldn't be provided government quarters as an E-1 or E-2, unless you're married, but the possibilities go up that you'll be able to live on your own after you make E-3.

Three meals a day is also a part of your pay package. You can eat three meals a day every day of the year in the mess hall—good, hearty, appetizing meals despite what you may have heard. But once again, if you have permission to live on your own, either in married quarters or off the base, you'll also draw a subsistence or ration allowance. This is the same for all enlisted grades, but the amount you get depends on whether you requested and were granted permission not to use the mess hall, or, for some reason, a mess hall isn't available where you are stationed. If you asked for permission, the rate is $3.21 a day, or an extra $96.30 in the average 30-day month. If no mess is available, then the rate is either $3.62 or $4.79 a day, depending on the situation. That's over a hundred dollars for food a month.

There's no regular mess hall for officers, so all officers are automatically paid $67.21 a month subsistence allowance.

There's also a clothing allowance for enlisted personnel. You'll be given your first uniforms, but after basic training you may either be given replacement uniforms on an exchange basis, that is, a new one for an old one, or be given a cash allowance to help pay for laundry, cleaning, and replacement as well as for new uniforms when you need them. A cash allowance is more routine than the exchange. This allowance varies with both service and sex—and here the women have the edge. It ranges from around $5 up to about $10 a month. Right now the highest allowance goes to a female Marine.

Officers get an initial allowance to buy their first uniforms, and from then on they are on their own.

If you are an enlisted man assigned to certain special duties that require special uniforms or an increase in the number of uniforms, such as a Marine on embassy duty or some band members, you'll receive a lump-sum allowance for the extras. You can also get a lump-sum allowance for buying civilian clothes if you go into intelligence or military police work that requires you to wear civvies instead of a uniform.

EXTRA PAY

First you get base pay, then allowances, and now we'll look at a number of ways you can put still more dollars in your paycheck.

Incentive Pay for Hazardous Duty. This is given to you if you perform duties that involve dangers not encountered in ordinary military jobs. If you are an enlisted crew member of an aircraft or a submarine, you'll receive an extra $50 to $105 a month, depending on your pay grade and time in service. If you join a parachute unit and make jumps or make frequent aerial flights not as a crew member, you can earn $55 extra a month. The same is true if you work on an aircraft-carrier flight deck, become a demolitions expert, or volunteer to be a guinea pig in certain medical experiments, such as stress tests. Diving pay, varying from $65 to $110 a month, is paid to qualified enlisted divers, based on rating and the type of diving performed.

You can receive two types of hazardous duty pay at the same time. For example, an airborne demolitions man earns $110 a month extra.

Officers can also earn extra pay, from $110 a month for hazardous duty to up to $245 a month for flight pay.

Sea and Foreign Duty Pay. This is authorized whenever you are on sea duty or while stationed in certain places overseas where you have extremes in climate or where the facilities are not up to standard. This starts at $8 a month for an E-1 and goes up to $22.50 for an E-7 or higher. It's not much, but it's nontaxable, and it adds up in time.

Hostile-Fire Pay. This is the pay that no one wants to become eligible for, but it's also the ultimate reason for the existence of our armed services. If you are in a hostile-fire area, you'll get an extra $65 a month. This means not just the troops in the combat line but anyone in the combat area, which could be a whole country or even several countries.

Now let's make up a hypothetical you and see what you could earn if you combined these factors.

Let's say you are single, have been in just over two years, are an E-3 in an Army airborne unit, and have permission to live off base. To start, you'd draw $548 base pay, plus $110 quarters allowance, about $96 ration allowance, and at least $5 clothing allowance. Added to all that would be $55 a month hazardous-duty pay. It rounds to about $814, of which $211 is tax-free.

Not bad for two years' service. And there's still more in the offing.

Extra Pay You Can Earn Later

Proficiency Pay is what the services give you if you are proficient in a skill that they need badly. You have to be in the service awhile to earn this, because it takes time to develop the skill levels required, but it's nice to know that if you do become a highly skilled specialist you can earn up to $150 more a month. This is the military's way of trying to keep you from leaving the service and marketing the skill they gave you in the civilian market.

Bonuses are another way the services try to hang on to people with critical skills. They are normally paid you when you reenlist. They may be a flat fee or be based on a formula such as a month's base pay for each year you sign up for. In other words, a six-year reenlistment would mean a bonus of six months' base pay. And if you've developed a really highly critical skill, for instance, if you are a nuclear-submarine crew member, you might qualify for special-skill bonuses of up to $15,000 for a six-year enlistment.

These bonuses change all the time as the needs of the services change and fluctuate with supply and demand, but there are usually some available all the time. Therefore, when you enter the service, find out about the current ones, and if you want to earn any of them, steer your career in that direction.

That should give you some idea of the pay you may earn after you've been in for a few years. And there are still others. There are allowances and extra pay for all types of situations, such as official travel, moving your family, living in temporary quarters, being separated from your family for extended periods of time, and even an extra cost-of-living allowance if you're assigned to some high-priced areas overseas.

You'll learn about them when you're in the service and the situation arises that authorizes the pay.

. . . WITH THE FRINGE ON TOP

As a smart job hunter you shouldn't look just at the salary offered; you should also take a close look at the extras. Does your employer offer paid vacations, hospitalization and other insurance, paid travel, free training, a retirement plan, or what?

These are called fringe benefits, and they can add a lot to the value of your pay package. And that's what you are looking for: a pay package, not just a salary. Your employer figures how much fringe benefits will cost him when he hires you, and you should think in terms of how much they are worth to you. In a good company the fringes can be worth as much as your salary, especially when you're just starting out. These salary-stretching extras can make the difference between just surviving and having a real vital life-style.

There's little argument against the fact that the military offers the biggest and best package deal available today for the low man on the totem pole—who is you. After you've been in awhile and have acquired a skill, you might find something equal or better outside the military, but you'll have to search for it.

The military's list of fringe benefits is very long. A complete explanation of all of them would take a book the size of this one, so all that will be covered here are the most important ones. Once again, after you enlist you'll learn all you need to know about them. And it's only then that you can decide how valuable each one is to you, because the value will depend on how much you use them.

Medical and Dental Care. You'll get complete medical and dental coverage at no cost, and if you do get sick you'll draw your full pay even if your illness requires extended hospitalization. Your dependents will get full medical care too, but dental care for dependents is provided only in emergencies.

If you must use a civilian doctor or hospital, you'll get about 80 percent of the bill paid, but you can take out inexpensive insurance to cover the rest. If you have any idea of the cost of health care in the civilian world, you'll be able to see how valuable this benefit could be if you or a dependent became seriously ill or had an accident.

Thirty Days' Leave Every Year. In private industry you

would have to be on the job a long time before you could expect to get even two or three weeks' vacation. But in the military everyone, from recruit to general, gets thirty days' leave every year. You earn this at a rate of 2½ vacation days a month, and it's possible to take leave before you've really earned it. You may also earn passes or liberties of up to three days that don't count against your leave time. In addition, you get off all national holidays, and if you work on a holiday you can expect to be given the equivalent time off later.

Travel. If you've ever wanted to see the world, the military will be glad to oblige. It may be a brief trip on military business or an assignment for several years, but either way you'll get a chance to see new places and meet new people. Of course, some of the places may not be to your liking, but even in the worst areas you will be close enough to some interesting place where you can go on a leave or pass. And even if you take a trip on your own, being in the military can help, because commercial carriers, such as the airlines, often offer special discounts to the military. You are also eligible for military-space-available travel (called Space-A). Space available means you can have any seat—free—on a military transport that is not filled by someone traveling on orders. You can do this on the transport planes of all the services, regardless of which uniform you wear, and that means it is possible to go almost anywhere in the world. These seats are not easy to get, and you'll have to wait and take your chances on them, but they are there if you want to try for them.

Low-Cost Life Insurance. This probably doesn't mean much to you now if you're young and single, but the services offer a group policy called Servicemen's Group Life Insurance (SGLI) that gives you $20,000 coverage for only $3.40 a month. The services think this is so important that you are automatically insured on this policy as soon as you enlist, and the premium is automatically deducted from your pay unless you state in writing—they'll provide you with the opportunity and the form—that you don't want it. You don't have to take it all. You can get coverage in $5000 pieces for 85 cents each month. If you're married or have a dependent parent, this is a good deal. Even if you're still single it's something to think about in your long-range financial planning. The future will come faster than you think.

Commissaries and Exchanges. A commissary is like a supermarket, and an exchange can be compared to a department store. Most installations have them, and the bigger the base is, the bigger are the commissary and exchange. You can make substantial savings by shopping in these stores, because they operate at a much lower mark-up than civilian stores. It has been estimated that if you did all your grocery and household shopping in the commissary, for example, you'd save at least 20 percent over what the same purchases would cost you in a civilian supermarket. In other words, your ten dollars would buy what would cost you about twelve dollars off base, or your fifty dollars would buy sixty dollars' worth. And since these stores are on federal property, they are exempt from state or local sales taxes. That alone could save you an additional 5 percent or more. Admittedly, sometimes discount stores can undersell the commissary and exchange on certain items, but not on the full range of merchandise.

Educational Benefits. This is such a big part of your military pay package that it's covered in a separate chapter called "The Big Red, White, and Blue Schoolhouse." But briefly, if you have any plans for continuing your education, the military offers a lot of help. In addition to the 10 percent or more of your time you'll probably spend in military schools, the services offer a continuing education package that few civilian employers could afford to offer you. Whether you want to take a G.E.D. (Graduate Equivalency Diploma) or go on for your Ph.D., the services have a program for you. And most of these programs are available to you in one form or another, no matter where you're stationed or what your duties. If you enlist and decide to try to take a big step up in your career and become an officer, each service has an educational program for that too.

Enlisted Members' and Officers' Clubs. As an enlisted member of the services you'll find that there are free clubs that offer you low-cost entertainment, social programs, food and beverage services, fun classes, and a place to relax away from the daily routine. These clubs are part of the worldwide recreation programs the services run. They are usually just for the lower grades. When you get some rank you'll be able to join other clubs just like them but restricted to NCOs or officers, but you'll have to pay dues to belong to those clubs. On the larger bases the enlisted clubs often feature name entertainers and musical groups to perform for dances or in concert. These clubs, and the service clubs, also provide other forms of recreation— everything from pool and Ping-Pong to mountain climbing and scuba diving.

Other Recreational Facilities. Whether you want to read, watch TV, go hunting or fishing, swim, ski—or whatever is your pleasure—the services probably have the facilities and equipment you need so you can do your thing. Just as an example, the Navy alone has more than

8400 recreational centers and facilities worldwide, not including what is on board the ships. These off-ship facilities include 65 golf courses, 1480 bowling centers, 250 swimming pools, over 1100 tennis courts, 52 marinas, 400 general recreation halls, 205 theaters, and 130 hobby shops. Organized athletic programs range from competition in all major sports between local groups right up to individual participation in the Olympics. And if you just want to shoot a few baskets or lift a few weights on your own, there's almost always a gym handy. In other words, the military has a stake in keeping you happy and in shape to do your job, and will offer you almost anything you need to let you do that. From libraries to flying clubs, from motorcross to painting, from do-it-yourself auto repair to sky diving: if you want it, they will get it for you.

Etc., Etc., Etc. The list goes on and on, so to wind up this chapter and get on with the career business, here's a partial list of some of the other benefits available to you free or at very low cost: legal and tax assistance, credit-union membership, payment for your suggestions, FHA in-service home loans, free elementary and high schools all over the world for your children, emergency financial grants and loans, talent and entertainment contests up to the national level, low-cost recreation centers in major tourist areas like Waikiki Beach, Hawaii, camping and travel-trailer parks, religious facilities and religious retreat areas, and all kinds of social and activity organizations such as drama clubs, CB clubs, and sports clubs.

Retirement. And finally, on the distant horizon, but still something you can see and are going toward each day, is the biggest fringe benefit of all—retirement at up to 75 percent of your final base pay.

A Summing Up. What does all this add up to?

If you work hard and give a dollar's worth of your labor and intelligence for a dollar's pay, your salary could easily double in a four-year hitch, and your allowances and fringe benefits could add half again to that, to give you the capability for a life-style far beyond what your equal civilian salary could buy.

And in addition to the money and other tangible benefits, there's an added reward you'll come to recognize. It's a reward too often scoffed at today—the reward of doing something for your country. You'll harvest the mental and emotional rewards of patriotism, honor, and service. The job of the military is to protect the people of our nation—and that includes the people who ridicule the military. They are able to ridicule the military only because their rights and freedoms are protected by it. When you get that feeling of pride at a parade or ceremony, or feel so good you're ready to burst after a difficult field exercise or test, then you'll know that those who ridicule patriotism don't really know the score. They'll never experience the surge of deep personal satisfaction that comes with the wearing of the uniform and being part of the 2 million men and women who have sworn to protect our way of life—an organization in arms to keep the peace.

CHAPTER THREE

"Female" Means Equal–Well, Almost

"Equal pay for equal work!"

That legitimate battle cry of women is answered in the military. Both work and pay are by rank and capabilities, not by sex. That's a fact, but it's a fact that sometimes gets a little foggy around the edges.

Women in the military are in the home stretch, but they still have a long way to go to cross the finish line of complete equality. If they had reached that point, this chapter wouldn't be necessary, because everything in this book would apply equally to men and women, instead of just most of it.

Women in the service do get equal pay for equal work. The problem is they still have a hard time getting the equal work, or holding on to it when they get it.

A PROGRESS REPORT

Let's look at the bright side first—and it gets brighter every day.

As recently as 1970, enlisted women could serve in only 35 percent of all military job specialties. Thus the number of specialties closed to women far outnumbered those open to them.

Now the reverse is true.

In the Air Force women may serve in 45 of 48 officer career programs and in all but seven of about 250 enlisted occupational specialties. The closed specialties are all combat jobs, but even there we can see a breakthrough. Women officers now have their fingers on the buttons that can launch a SAC H-bomb-tipped rocket at a target halfway around the world.

Enlistment, training, commissioning, and promotion rules in the Air Force are the same for women as for men.

In the Army, women may now be assigned to all but about 16 of the more than 300 enlisted occupational specialties. Although they can't be assigned to direct-combat jobs they are assigned to work in direct-combat support jobs. For example, some women are assigned to the nonfiring units of defensive missile outfits such as HAWK and Hercules air defense units. They also may fill all aviation-unit positions except those of an aerial scout or attack-helicopter crew. Women in the field on maneuvers with male troops are so commonplace now that the portable post exchanges that go with the troops not only carry *Playboy* and other male magazines but also routinely stock *Cosmopolitan* and *Woman's Day.*

Some enlisted basic training is still separate, but Army men and women take all advanced training together.

In the Navy men and women take their training together right from the start. Although women are restricted by law from serving aboard combat ships and aircraft, almost all other jobs are open to them, including sea duty aboard noncombat ships.

In 1979, only four combat career fields were still closed to women in the Marines. That service is in the process of wiping out its separate women's detachments and integrating women with the men for both duty and training.

Coast Guard policy calls for complete equality. It states that mixed-sex crews may be assigned to any unit afloat or ashore that can provide reasonable privacy in berthing and personnel-hygiene areas. Considering the small size of some Coast Guard ships, this may still restrict the use of mixed-sex crews, but the policy is there and women are moving forward.

All the military academies are now open to women cadets. Annapolis, the Air Force Academy, the Coast Guard Academy, and West Point first opened their doors to women in 1976, with the first women cadets in the class of 1980. In doing this they followed the lead of the U.S. Merchant Marine Academy, which was the first federal academy to admit women, in 1974. Women graduates from that school earn certificates as both deck and engineering officers in the Merchant Marine and are eligible for Naval Reserve commissions, just as male graduates are.

From the long-range view, perhaps what is even more important than the opening up of specialties to women is that more and more women are moving up to command positions in both the NCO and officer ranks. In these positions they will be in charge of units made up of both men and women.

The big breakthrough in this area came in 1970, when

the Army appointed the first two women brigadier generals (one star). The Air Force soon followed, appointing a woman general in 1971, and the Navy appointed the first woman rear admiral in 1972. A year later the Air Force broke another barrier by promoting a woman to two-star rank. These women aren't wearing stars just as a publicity gimmick either. They hold responsible positions. One of them, for example, is in command of Fort McClellan, Alabama, which is a major post and the Army's military-police training center.

A Touch of History

The history of women in the service is as old as our nation. In 1775, the Second Continental Congress authorized "that a matron be alloted for every hundred sick and wounded."

Unfortunately, that image of a "matron" carried on for almost two centuries. Even though the number of women in uniform in World War II reached a wartime high of almost 290,000, women were still considered just "matrons," traveling along as temporary passengers, who would get off when the war ended.

The history of these two centuries of women in the service is fascinating and enlightening, but of necessity is a subject for separate study. What we need to know here is that the military is no longer interested in temporary help from "matrons." They are all looking for full-time workers.

Why the Change of Heart?

In 1968, at the height of the Vietnam War, there were fewer than 40,000 women in uniform. In 1978 there were close to 120,000—three times the Vietnam number. And this was in time of peace.

The announced goal of the Department of Defense is to have 200,000 women in uniform by the early 1980's—in a total force of about 2 million.

Why this change of heart? Why has the military developed this sudden professional interest in women?

Like many subjects relating to defense, it boils down to simple economics: cost factors, supply and demand, and the long-range effects of the Pill.

The Cost Factors

Everyone who takes a pre-enlistment test falls into one of five intelligence categories labeled from I to V. None of the services want Category V people. They are too difficult and expensive to train. Most of the services will take a Category IV—but they aren't eager to do so. Category IV people are accepted for enlistment because it is felt that their brawn will make up for their shortage of brainpower. That means, of course, that a Category IV person *has* to have brawn, or he is not acceptable. There are still a number of military jobs where brawn can earn its way if it has good supervision and leadership.

Women in general, however, are not noted for their brawn, so they are slotted for jobs that require more intellectual skill and an ability to learn rather than muscle power. As a result, in the past women had to score high enough to get into Category III to be eligible to enlist.

It is a positive reflection on the improved status of women in our society that this change has taken place. And, of course, it is a clear indication that our armed services are "open" to all in terms of opportunity, and that they are flexible and moving with the times.

A high-school graduate scoring in Category III or above is considered a "high-quality" enlistee, one the services feel they can train and make fully productive. And here's where the cost factor first comes in. The services are finding it more and more difficult to find and enlist "high-quality" men. For one thing, they are also in demand in private industry. Adding the costs of recruiting staffs, advertising, and so on, the Air Force finds it comes close to $900 to sign up one "high-quality" male. That figure zooms to about $2000 for the Navy and $4000 for the Army.

On the other hand, it costs less than $200 to find and sign a Category IV male without a high-school diploma— or to sign up any eligible female.

Why does it cost so little for Group IV men? Because they find it hard to get jobs and so are eager to join.

Why does it cost so little to recruit a woman? Because the number of women needed by the services is still relatively small compared to the number of women in the job market. And also because there are a lot of female high-school graduates out there who can see that the military offers them a better start on almost any career than private industry, and at a better starting pay.

Statistics show that the *average* woman with a high-school diploma can make about $2000 more a year in the military than she would starting out in the civilian work world. And if she has a college degree and becomes an officer, she can make, on the average, about $3000 more a year in the military right at the start. As she gets older and more experienced, the difference is even greater. This is primarily because the chance for advancement is better in the military than in the average civilian job.

Of course, those recruiting costs will go up as the number of women in the military gets closer to the goal of 200,000 and the female labor pool becomes harder to dip into. But by that time the other reasons why the military wants women enlistees will come into play to make it worthwhile to pay higher recruiting costs.

The next statistic in favor of women in uniform is that research indicates they are more productive than men over the long run, because they lose less time from their jobs. Now remember, this is a broad-based statistic. It's not a case of one man's record versus one woman's, but servicemen in general versus servicewomen in general. And, in general, the records show that men are more likely to lose time because of problems with alcohol and drug abuse as well as punishment for breaking the rules. Women, on the other hand, generally lose most of their work time because of pregnancy—but the services seem to agree that that's the price they must pay to have women in uniform, and they're willing to live with it.

Another statistic in favor of women is that they have a slightly higher reenlistment rate than men. This is not a significant figure, but once the services have spent money to train people they don't want to lose them and the skills they have learned. It seems that more men decide to try their new skills in the civilian world than do women, and every skilled person who leaves means money and time to train someone else all over again.

So much for a quick rundown on the cost factors. Now let's look at an even more important statistic—population decline, and its effect on supply and demand.

Supply and Demand—and the Pill

A main effect of the Pill was the end of the baby boom. As a result, in the mid 1980's there will be a 15 percent drop in the supply of 18-year-old males and, by the 1990's, a 25 percent drop. Since 18-year-old males are the main source of enlistments, and since the military has a demand for about a thousand enlistees a day to maintain its strength at about 2 million, it's going to get harder and harder and more and more expensive for the services to enlist "high-quality" men.

There are three ways to solve the problem: (1) to make the military so attractive that young men will beat down the doors to enlist; (2) return to the draft, or (3) fill the shortages with women. The military is working on making the services more attractive all the time—as you can see from the rest of this book—but to go all out would wreck the national budget and probably still not get enough healthy young men into uniform. The draft is not a dead issue. By the time you read this, draft registration may once again be required by law—perhaps even for women—but there's still a lot of political opposition to a full-fledged draft. So the best solution, and the one the services have all adopted, is to open the doors wide to women.

What does this all add up to?

Opportunity for any woman who wants a pick of jobs in the military (not to mention the opportunity to meet "high-quality" men).

Some Problems

As already mentioned, most of the information and advice in this book applies equally to both sexes, but there are a few problems that apply only to women.

These problems aren't being presented here to scare you off. On the contrary, they are presented to make sure you have the complete picture. If you are aware of a problem before you run into it, you will be better prepared to cope with it if it happens to arise.

The first problem is your physical fitness.

Basic training is not easy. Depending on the service, you'll have to be prepared for six to ten weeks of fairly strenuous physical exercise and programs that run from early in the morning to late in the evening. If you took physical-fitness classes in high school, and they made you work up a good sweat, you probably won't have any trouble. But if you didn't, you'd be wise to get yourself in shape before you are sent to the basic-training center.

In most services you will be taking basic training with the male recruits. About the only thing you'll find modified to help you are the physical-training requirements—but they haven't been modified much. The military has found that the average woman recruit is fully capable of doing most of what the men have to do, including the man-style push-up. So you'll be expected to run, just not as fast, and do sit-ups and push-ups, just not as many.

The next place your physical fitness comes to bear is in your choice of a job.

If you really want to do something out of the ordinary—a nontraditional job, as the services put it—you'll be given the opportunity. You can try to be anything from an asphalt equipment operator to a welder. Not only will they offer you the chance, they'll encourage you to go into nontraditional jobs. These jobs are especially wide open, because most women, even when given the chance, have shied away from them, preferring to stick with the traditional jobs. If a different job appeals to you, make sure you ask your recruiter about the physical demands of the job before you get too deeply involved. You should be aware that if you think you'd get a kick out of being a telephone lineman, it involves more than just being able to climb a pole. It involves being able to climb a pole with a pack of heavy equipment or a load of cable.

If you feel you have the strength and stamina and the interest, you can get almost any job you want. But if you don't think you'd be comfortable in a nontraditional job, even though you lean that way, you might start out in a traditional one—in the fields of administration, medicine, communications, or intelligence, for example—and then, after you've been in the service a little while and know your way around, you can still decide you want to operate a bulldozer or work on a tugboat and ask for a transfer.

The next problem is that you are moving into what not so long ago was strictly a man's world. It's no longer "this man's Army," or this man's any other service, for that matter. However, many senior male NCO's and officers grew up in that all-male world and still are not prepared to welcome women in it. It's not that they are male chauvinists—although the macho image still reigns in the combat units—it's often simply that they just don't know what to do with you.

If you are the first woman assigned to a unit, or the first assigned to a nontraditional job in a unit, you will probably end up as office decoration no matter what your job is supposed to be. It isn't until several women are working there that these superiors suddenly realize they can't get their mission accomplished if they send all the women to sit in an office and brew coffee. When this knowledge hits them they'll reluctantly give in and put you to work at the job you were trained to do.

Even then your problem doesn't just go away. Initially, at least, you'll have to work harder than the new man next to you doing the same job, because the older hands won't accept you as an equal until you prove you are their equal in work. You won't have this trouble in traditional jobs, but you'll have to prove yourself to your co-workers if you tackle a nontraditional one. The rewards of acceptance will be well worth the effort, but be prepared to work hard for them.

Once again, the purpose of this discussion is not to scare you away from the nontraditional job, or to kill your dream, it's just to put you on your guard so you won't get discouraged and quit before you've given the job and yourself a chance.

Your Biological Problem

One of the biggest problems you might face won't be a problem if you understand that the military is enlisting you as a person to do a job, not as a female looking for a mate.

Not that they have anything against dating or getting married; in fact, free-time activities are set up to give you plenty of opportunity to do either or both. And if you are already married to a serviceman you might consider joining him officially by enlisting. It'll mean double pay, a good job, and benefits, and all the services have a policy of trying to station husbands and wives together.

What they are concerned about is that as a woman you are a biological hazard in that you are a potential child bearer. In other words, they are scared you'll get pregnant. The military looks at pregnancy as the greatest obstacle to full integration of women into the services. Not on moral grounds—that's your personal business—but strictly because a pregnant servicewoman is not capable of doing her duty.

Only a few years back, getting pregnant, married or not, meant automatic discharge for a servicewoman. Now a servicewoman who becomes pregnant has the choice of receiving an honorable discharge or of staying in and taking maternity leave and keeping her baby. And it doesn't matter if you are married or not. Single parents are accepted, but not encouraged.

If a pregnant woman chooses to stay in, she'll stay at her regular job as long as she's physically and medically able. There are even maternity uniforms now. If the job is too strenuous she may be assigned a temporary job with lighter duties until the doctor says she's ready for maternity leave.

What disturbs the services is that, for some women, maternity leave may mean up to four months away from the job and the unit—drawing full pay. This hurts the unit, and also creates a morale problem with the men, who resent it.

On the bright side, the pregnant servicewoman gets all her medical care and the delivery as part of her free medical benefits.

How big a problem is this? In one recent year 15 percent of the enlisted women in the Army became pregnant. Some of them were married, some not. The Air Force has estimated that doubling the number of enlisted women in that service by the early 1980's will mean about 5,500 pregnancies a year, and about 3000 of these mothers will remain on active duty with very young children. Whether they are married or not, it will result in excessive time off, assignment problems, and a fall-off in unit productivity.

The services are all giving serious thought to this growing problem (no pun intended), but for now seem willing to live with it—a clear indication of how desperately they need womanpower.

Servicewomen and Combat

There is a big debate going on as to whether or not women should be given combat assignments. In other words: Should all the restrictions be lifted and women given full equality?

Women fall in on both sides of this debate, just as they do in the wrangle over the Equal Rights Amendment. Those in favor of full equality cite the fact that during World War II more than a million Russian women were drafted into the armed forces, and many of them served in combat. Records show that Russian women served as fighter pilots, tank-crew members, machine gunners, on artillery crews, and as snipers. How true the stories of their exploits are is difficult to tell, but it is interesting to note that women serve only in traditional jobs in today's Soviet armed forces.

Everyone also knows that Israeli women fought in the 1948 war for independence, but, like the Russian women, they are not serving in combat units today.

And, of course, the proponents of giving combat roles to women also cite the reputation of the fierce women fighters in the Viet Cong during the Vietnamese War.

On the other hand, despite the heroics of the likes of

"Charlie's Angels," or their stunt doubles, the opponents claim that since the average woman doesn't have the strength or stamina of the average man she could not take sustained combat. Most military leaders, and also our political leaders, go along with this. So even if the legal restrictions are lifted, it will be a rare female who winds up in a Marine rifle squad or flying an Air Force fighter as full-time duty.

This does not mean the services are not willing to train women for combat. On the contrary, they are already doing it. But it is for defensive combat, not offensive. They are not being trained to take the battle to the enemy, but rather to defend themselves and their unit, as every serviceperson must, if the enemy comes to them.

The guerrilla warfare in Vietnam showed that front lines in combat are no longer easily defined. If another war comes—big or small—we can expect massive parachute and helicopter assaults and/or guerrilla attacks behind the lines. Then everyone—clerks, mechanics, cooks, computer operators—must be able to face and fight the enemy.

But what is perhaps more likely than a war is the continuing threat of worldwide terrorism, which can make any spot a battleground.

One of the first things the military did to prepare women for this eventuality was to lift the restriction on training them in small arms. As expected, both officers and enlisted women have often proved to be excellent marksmen—or markswomen. The old cowboy movie cliché of the womenfolk loading rifles while the men fight off the bad guys is now a thing of the past.

Eventually some of the services started giving women the same basic training as men, including combat training.

Women second lieutenants in the Marines now take the same 21-week basic officer training as the new male officers. This means they spend a lot of time in the field, go on forced marches with 50-pound packs, sleep in the rain and freezing weather, and fire all the weapons they would have to be familiar with if they were in an infantry platoon. The Marines decided to do this not just so the women would be able to defend themselves, but also so that in time of combat they would understand what the combat soldier was going through, even if the women themselves were in relatively safe jobs.

The Army is doing the same with enlisted women. They are gradually eliminating separate basic training for women and putting them through the regular basic combat training program.

All this might be compared to teaching a woman karate. She isn't expected to use this martial art to enforce her will on the world, but rather to be able to protect herself from the mugger or rapist who would bring violence to her.

Considering that combat is the basic reason for the existence of our armed forces, women may never reach—or even want—full equality.

A Brief Summing-Up

On the whole, women are closer to equality and have more career opportunities in the military than they will find in private industry. And even though there are special problems that women must be aware of when they enter the service, they will find similar problems in civilian life. In addition, in the world of civilian work, women are more often forced to work below their potential and without equal pay for equal work.

Overall, the military offers an interesting and maturing experience, expert training for a civilian or military career, and many benefits for any woman willing to meet the challenge.

The key question is: Do you really want a slice of this action? If you do, then the chances of getting the slice you want have never been better.

CHAPTER 4

Introducing the Five Different Services

Gary brings his fighter in for a landing on the aircraft carrier. Is he a Navy pilot? No, he wears the globe and anchor of the Marines.

Helen heads her landing craft through the surf toward the beach. Is she a Navy or Coast Guard boatswain? No, she is a watercraft operator in an Army transportation unit.

Paul stands in the door of a troop-carrier aircraft and waits for the green light to tell him to jump. An Army airborne trooper? No, he is a member of an Air Force combat control team.

Carlos lowers the blade on a bulldozer and starts to level a hill. An Army combat engineer? No, he is a member of a Navy construction battalion.

And so it goes. It's hard to tell the players without their

uniforms. Within the services the duplication of even such specialized jobs as these is widespread. There are hundreds of similar jobs in different services, called by different names but with the same basic duties. A cook may be called a cook in the Air Force and Marines, a food-service specialist in the Army, a subsistence specialist in the Coast Guard, and a mess management specialist in the Navy, but in all the services his or her job is still basically the same. A cook is a cook, a clerk-typist is a clerk-typist, and an auto mechanic is an auto mechanic, no matter what name the service tacks on to the job.

Duplication Means Opportunity

So what does this mean to you?

It means more opportunities. The fact that there is duplication in jobs among the services is to your benefit. It means that if you can't get the job you want in the service you want, you still have a chance for it in one of the other services.

If there is so much duplication, and if everyone in the same pay grade gets the same base pay in every service, does it really matter which service you join?

It sure does, because each service has a different mission, a different reason for its existence. Each service specializes in some form of warfare or peacekeeping, and that specialization sets it apart from the others. That specialized mission also normally molds the life-styles of the people in that service.

It's important that you understand these missions and a little about each of the services before you make your decision about which one you want to join.

THE UNITED STATES AIR FORCE

Our Air Force is assigned the mission of being always ready for sustained combat in the air.

What does that mean? It means the Air Force must be fully trained and ready at all times to make sure that in the event of war we rule the skies. A tall order!

Air combat these days doesn't just mean two pilots dogfighting their planes over the combat zone. It also includes the crew in an underground silo in the Midwest, who must be ready to fire a giant nuclear warheaded missile at a target half the world away. It means sweeping the skies of enemy bombers before they can strike our cities, providing close air support to our combat forces on land and sea, and providing air transport for the rapid movement of troops and supplies to trouble spots all over the world. Those are a few of the things involved in the Air Force mission.

The Air Force might also be called the Space Force, because it is also charged with developing new military space projects. This involves the research and development of all United States military satellites and includes military space probes and space weapons that can destroy enemy space weapons and satellites. The sky's no longer the limit for the Air Force; only the galaxy is.

To carry out all these jobs the Air Force has somewhat fewer than 600,000 full-time personnel, about 7,000 aircraft, and approximately 140 major installations and thousands of smaller facilities in the United States and in about twenty-four friendly countries.

As with all the services, the overall mission is divided into separate parts, which are assigned to various subordinate commands. The major subordinate commands of the Air Force include:

The Strategic Air Command (SAC), which operates our main air-strike force using manned long-range bombers and intercontinental missiles.

The Tactical Air Command (TAC), which provides the tactical fighters to oppose attacking enemy aircraft, provides close support to our combat troops, and gives us superiority in the air.

The Military Airlift Command (MAC), which provides transports to airlift troops and supplies to any spot on the globe.

The Air Training Command (ATC), which will be your first official contact with the Air Force, since it is responsible for the recruitment and training of all AF personnel.

And there are other commands, such as the U.S. Air Forces in Europe and the Pacific Air Forces.

Impact on Your Life-style

Perhaps someday space stations will overcome the laws of gravity, but until then all aircraft that go up must eventually come down. And therefore, the place where the plane goes up and comes down—the air base—will be the center of your life. With the increasing size and technological complexity of aircraft, the air base has also had to increase in size and complexity to support these winged computers, and in order to support the people who support the aircraft, bases have become small towns with all the niceties—housing developments, lawns, restaurants, stores, libraries, schools, banks, gas stations, bowling alleys, clubs, tennis courts, swimming pools, fire stations, and churches.

With few exceptions, most Air Force personnel live on or near the air base on which they work. In the Air Force the air base is the center of your work as well as your life-style. AF personnel rarely go to the field. Even the combat air crews operate out of a base. That is why the Air Force is known by the combat personnel of the other services—perhaps with a touch of envy—as the service where you can come home to clean beds, flush toilets, and a cold drink after a hard day at the war. (The flush toilets may not always be true, but the rest usually is, even at an advanced fighter base.)

Your tour of duty at a base—that is, the length of time you can expect to be assigned to work there—depends on your job and the location of the base itself. The tour of duty at a base in the United States ranges from two to five years. Overseas it is normally from one to three years, depending on such things as the desirability of the area (a mountaintop communications site in Turkey or a base in Italy), the facilities available (with or without all the comforts of home), and whether or not married airmen or airwomen can bring their families to the area. However, either in the States or overseas, if you like it where you are and the Air Force likes the job you're doing, you can ask for an extension of time on your tour and stay there another year or longer.

Flying or Nonflying Jobs

There is a dividing line between life-styles in the Air Force that is so distinct it is almost visible. The line is drawn between those who fly and those who don't.

On the flying side you'll have a tough but interesting job with a coating of adventure. On the other side of the line, you'll find your job is usually an interesting one too, but don't expect much in the way of adventure in your work.

Personnel on flying status put their lives on the line every time they take off in an aircraft. This fact is recognized in all the services, and so all flight crews receive extra pay—flight pay—for doing it.

Pilots and flight crews may be here today and halfway around the world tomorrow. Those assigned to combat units like SAC or TAC can expect long periods of "temporary duty" (called by the initials TDY) at another base. A TDY may last from overnight to several months. But even at a TDY base you'll probably have all the comforts of home.

If you have a nonflying job you can expect a life-style not unlike that of civilians working on the base. You'll get up, go to work at the base, put in regular hours, come home, and spend your off-duty hours doing your thing. If you want adventure it may be available outside your job. You might want to become involved in some adventurous recreation program, such as hang gliding. Even for those not seeking adventure, there's a whole new world of experiences waiting outside the gates of the base, especially if the base is in some place like West Berlin, Spain, or an island in the Caribbean.

Air Force nonflying personnel can usually look forward to a life free of most of the violent ups and downs and twists and turns of members of the other services. So if you want a predictable, steady life relatively free of inconveniences, the Air Force might be what you are looking for.

A Moment in Time in the Air Force

Let's see what a number of Air Force personnel might be doing at any one moment all around the world.

In the control tower at an airbase in Delaware, Airman First Class Beatrice Guerrero, an air-traffic controller, gives permission to the pilot of a C5A, one of the world's largest transports, to take off on a flight to the Middle East.

In Colorado, Airman First Class Janet Mabley, refrigeration and air-conditioning specialist, climbs in among the huge pipes and tubing of the plant supplying the air to the underground command center and checks to make sure there are no leaks.

At a TAC base in California, First Lieutenant Harold Anderson pushes the throttle in his F-16 fighter to full afterburner, and 25,000 pounds of thrust from his jet engines skyrocket the plane into the air.

At Hickam Field in Hawaii, Airman First Class Ophelia Thomas, weather observer, launches a pilot balloon she'll use in her weather forecasting.

In Moscow, Technical Sergeant Leon Hill, communications center specialist, is in the midst of encoding and sending a message from the Air Attaché to Air Force Headquarters in the Pentagon.

And First Lieutenant Lloyd Robinson, navigator, checks the course heading with the pilot as their B-52 heads for a rendezvous with an in-flight refueling aircraft north of the Azores.

THE UNITED STATES ARMY

The Army is the largest member of our armed forces. Its mission is to be always ready for sustained combat operations on land. The Army must be organized and trained, so it can take on and defeat an enemy land force and seize, occupy, and defend land areas.

That means it must be ready and able to fight in any part of the world, in any climate, at any time. Because of this, many of the Army's combat units and the units that immediately support them are stationed overseas near potential trouble spots.

At home, the Army has some peaceful missions too, such as those given to the Corps of Engineers to improve navigation on inland waterways and to build dams for flood control.

The Army has close to 800,000 men and women on active duty.

The major commands of the Army in the United States are:

The Training and Doctrine Command (TRADOC), which is responsible for all the training at the Army training centers—including basic training—and in the service schools.

The Forces Command (FORSCOM), which takes over when you leave training and are assigned to a unit. It is responsible for the combat readiness of all combat and combat support forces in the United States.

The Army Materiél Command, which is responsible for all the equipment the Army uses. That means it designs, buys, distributes, and teaches people to maintain everything from uniforms to tanks, from bullets to helicopters.

Impact on Your Life-Style

Until recently, the Army was considered the least glamorous of the services. Perhaps that was because it was always the largest service and so had to fill its ranks with reluctant draftees, who had bad-mouthed it at every chance, whereas the other services were able to fill up with volunteers—many volunteering to avoid being drafted into the Army. Or perhaps it was because the Army has had a reputation for preferring brawn to brains.

Neither of these reasons is valid today. Now all the armed forces are manned by volunteers, and eight out of ten jobs in today's Army require technical training comparable to that given in the other services. Even the much-put-down infantryman must be smart enough today to handle sophisticated weapons systems using electronics, lasers, and other complex components. Because of the glamour of these jobs, the Army is beginning to hold its own in getting qualified recruits.

Army posts, like Air Force bases, are located all over the United States and the free world, and are as fully equipped with all the comforts and facilities as the bases of any other service. Most Army posts are located either near a large training or maneuver area or in a place that was originally a frontier post a hundred years or more ago. In many cases cities have grown up around these older posts. Fort Sam Houston, Texas, for example, is near downtown San Antonio, and Fort Shafter, Hawaii, is not far from downtown Honolulu.

There is a dividing line in the Army much like the flying/nonflying line in the Air Force. In this case, it is between the troops in combat units who spend a great deal of time living and working in the field, and those in noncombat units who, like Air Force nonflyers, live and work on posts. But you'll find the dividing line is not as distinct because of the way the Army is organized.

The Army is broken down into branches. These

branches are classified by their mission: combat arms, technical services, and administrative services. The technical services include the Signal Corps and the Corps of Engineers; the administrative services include the Finance Corps, which handles all the Army's money, including your pay, and the Adjutants General Corps, which handles all the paperwork.

The blurring occurs because the Army's main combat organization is the division, with a strength of about 15,000 men. A division must be able to take care of itself in the field. It must have its own communications, engineer support, and transportation support; the troops must get paid, and the paperwork must get done. So in addition to the infantry, armor, and artillery units in the division, there are many support troops from the technical and administrative branches.

If you decide the Army is for you, you can expect you will spend some time in the field, no matter what your branch or specialty. If you choose one of the combat arms you'll spend most of your time in the field.

But don't look at this as a negative side of Army life. Living for a time without creature comforts can be a distinct pleasure, as hunters and fishermen know. It gets you out of the polluted air and, what is even more important, out of the garrison rut. You'll find that living and working in the field perfecting the teamwork of your unit can be an exhilarating job, though it may be physically and mentally demanding. It can instill in you a professional pride, as well as a personal pride in your own ability to meet and vanquish a demanding task, far outweighing the minor inconveniences.

And even combat units have a home and spend time in garrison. It's not all living in the great outdoors.

When you are on post you can expect to have a life-style roughly comparable to a civilian worker's. But you'll have things available to you that few civilian workers can brag about—the fringe benefits of low-cost entertainment, recreation, and education.

Army tours of duty range from a year at what is called an "undesirable" location to about three years at a good or "desirable" spot. As with the Air Force, and all the services, if you're doing a good job and want to stay where you are, you can ask for an extension of time on your tour and probably get it. The military doesn't want to move you any more often than it has to.

A Moment in Time in the Army

At Fort Benning, Georgia, Private Mark Chapa checks his parachute and starts to climb aboard an Air Force troop transport that will take him and his class up for their first night jump in the final week of training at the Army's Airborne School.

At Fort Knox, Kentucky, Private First Class (called by the initials PFC) Vickie Sobotik, finance specialist, is in her off-duty class in college-level accounting at the post education center.

At Fort Carson, Colorado, Warrant Officer Patricia Verdura, pilot, races to her helicopter to join a search-and-rescue mission for a climbing party lost in the nearby mountains.

In Alaska, Specialist 4 Rudy Costanza, helicopter mechanic, troubleshoots the engine of a helicopter to make certain it's ready to fly the next morning.

In Korea, PFC Debra Kaiser, office-machine repairperson, finishes fixing a typewriter in the headquarters of an artillery unit.

At a training area in West Germany, Corporal Fernando Ruiz, tank crewman, starts the motor on his tank and prepares for a black-out move to a position for a dawn attack on the units playing the enemy in a training exercise.

THE UNITED STATES COAST GUARD

The Coast Guard might be called the humanitarian service, because its basic mission is to protect man from the sea, the "sea" in this case meaning all bodies of water, including the Great Lakes and our major rivers. If you add up all the shorelines and riverbanks, the Coast Guard has the responsibility for over forty thousand miles of shore.

To carry out its mission the Coast Guard uses about 340 large cutters and other ships and hundreds of small craft and over 150 aircraft. With these it performs its jobs of search and rescue, enforces maritime safety laws and other laws on the sea, provides and maintains aids to navigation, operates ocean weather stations, studies oceanography, and participates in international ice patrols and ice-breaking duties.

In addition to helping man survive the sea, the Coast Guard also has the mission of helping the sea survive man. It has environmental duties that include the prevention of pollution and the cleaning up of oil spills.

There are about 38,000 men and women in this, the smallest of the nation's military services, and the only one under the Department of Transportation. (It comes under the control of the Navy in time of war or whenever the President so directs.)

The Coast Guard has divided the United States into twelve areas or districts. Each district is a major command headquarters. Although most of the Coast Guard's activities take place in the waters of the United States, some activities range into the Caribbean and as far away as Australia and the South Pole.

Impact on Your Life-style

If you join the Coast Guard, the odds are you'll be stationed along the Atlantic, Pacific, or Gulf coasts or on one of the Great Lakes. There are some stations inland and a few overseas, but very few.

You'll also spend a lot of time at sea, or, at least, on the water.

Since the Cost Guard is our smallest service, it follows that its bases are also small. Most are just a base for the crews of a cutter or two and some support personnel, or a lifeboat station with fewer than a hundred personnel. You'll find these smaller stations still provide off-duty activities, but on a limited scale. Fortunately, the mission requires that a number of Coast Guard installations be located in the harbors of major cities or in resort areas where pleasure boating is popular, and in these areas you'll find plenty of off-duty activities available off base. Other missions, however, require personnel to be assigned to isolated posts, and sometimes the group may have to make its own off-duty amusements.

Size also affects training. You'll be trained as a skilled

technician in one field and cross-trained in other fields, so you'll be able to fill in when a skilled man isn't available or one isn't assigned to your ship or boat.

A unique situation exists for Coast Guard personnel because of its law-enforcement duties. Once you have achieved your specialty and earned the rank of E-4, you automatically become a federal marshal.

A good point about being in this small service is that you are a person, not a number. You'll find more of the small-team or family atmosphere in both on- and off-duty time, in contrast to the "lost-in-the-crowd" feeling you might experience on a large base in one of the other services.

Coast Guard tours of duty at one location vary in length from one to four years, depending on the desirability of the station. Most short tours are at isolated stations, like the Long-Range-Aid-to-Navigation (LORAN) station at French Frigate Shoals, a small atoll in the middle of the Pacific. Isolated-area tours normally earn you extra pay and extra leave time at the end of the tour.

Sea duty may range from a cruise of several months aboard a 400-foot icebreaker or a 378-foot cutter on an oceanographic research voyage to a day on a 30-footer checking safety devices on pleasure craft.

Life aboard a large cutter at sea is about the same as it would be if you were on a Navy ship, except that you aren't training for a possible war but are on a working ship with a day-to-day job. The Coast Guard is the only service with a full-time peacetime mission.

In a recent year, for instance, the Coast Guard was credited with answering almost 80,000 calls for help, preventing about 4,200 deaths, assisting more than 125,000 people, and saving property valued at about $300 million.

A Moment in Time in the Coast Guard

About 150 miles off the coast of Massachusetts, Lieutenant Roy Povell and two armed Coast Guardsmen and two agents of the National Maritime Fisheries Service scamper up the rope ladder of a Russian fishing trawler suspected of violating the United States' 200-mile fishing zone.

Off the coast of Florida, Seaman Michael Reiger, radarman, is following the movements of a powerboat on his radar screen as the cutter he is on speeds to intercept. The powerboat is suspected of carrying a cargo of cocaine.

In Bay St. Louis, Mississippi, Petty Officer First Class Ken Bosley, diver, gets ready to join the other members of the 20-member Gulf Strike Team who will board a stricken oil tanker and try to prevent it from creating an oil spill.

At a lifeboat station in Oregon, Petty Officer First Class Barry McKnight, boatswain, steers his 44-foot self-bailing, self-righting motor lifeboat through heavy seas to reach the passengers of a small pleasure boat in distress.

At the lonely LORAN station on a tiny atoll in mid-Pacific, Petty Officer Third Class Tom Mieske, electronics technician, repairs one of the sophisticated transmitters that are part of the station's equipment to aid navigation.

THE UNITED STATES MARINE CORPS

The Marines are the "soldiers of the sea."

Although technically a part of the Department of the Navy, they are considered a separate service.

The Marines are a ground force, much like the Army, except they are specially trained and equipped to conduct ship-to-shore (amphibious) operations. Marine assault troops, supported by naval gunfire and Navy and Marine air cover, attack and seize enemy beachheads and bases. Once ashore, they operate much as the Army does except that certain support functions, such as medical, are provided by the Navy.

To carry out this mission, the Marines have Fleet Marine Forces (FMFs) with the various Navy fleets operating all over the world, which are ready to conduct over-the-beach and helicopter landing operations on short notice. These forces afloat are controlled by the two major headquarters, FMF Atlantic and FMF Pacific. A major portion of the Marines' total strength of about 190,000 is devoted to the three divisions and three Aircraft Wings that make up the FMFs and their support troops.

Those not assigned to FMF jobs carry out such duties as providing detachments for guard and other service aboard warships and the protection of naval bases and stations. Marines also guard all of the more than one hundred United States embassies, legations, and consulates around the world, as well as the President when he is at Camp David.

Impact on Your Life-style

The Marine reputation for being a tough outfit is well deserved. They still are tough, but like the ground-pounding Army, the Marines have been caught up in the technological revolution, and it is no longer a service of just muscle power and bellowing sergeants. Jobs are available in thirty-nine career fields, and most of them require technical training.

Marine combat units spend a great deal of time training in the field—or on the beach. If you join the Marines, your chances of being assigned to a combat unit are high, because that's where most Marines work.

Although there are a lot of similarities between the Army and the Marines, the Marines emphasize that a main difference is the stress the Corps places on high standards of discipline, physical fitness, and unit and self-pride.

Because it is a sea service, Marine bases are concentrated on the Atlantic and Pacific coasts, but they also have some bases overseas. Marine bases offer all the off-duty facilities found on the bases of the other services. However, because of their interest in physical fitness, the recreational emphasis is usually heavy on active sports programs.

Stateside tours range from one to five years, overseas tours from one to three years. Unlike the Army, Marines are rarely authorized to move their families to an overseas base even if the other services class the area as desirable. Marine families normally remain at bases in the States, so the troops overseas can maintain a high state of combat readiness and not have to worry about their dependents in an emergency.

A Moment in Time in the Marine Corps

Aboard a nuclear carrier in the Gulf of Mexico, Lance Corporal Randall Hobbs is on guard duty on the ship's bridge.

At Camp Pendleton, California, Corporal Randy Corne, HAWK missile system operator, helps his fellow crew members pack up and get ready to return to camp after a night training exercise.

At Kaneohe, Hawaii, Private First Class Audrey Blum, computer operator, working the night shift, changes a tape and prepares to start a new supply program.

Off the coast of Korea, First Lieutenant Bob Engel, pilot, and First Lieutenant Julien Romo, flight officer, fly their Phantom F-4 on a training mission.

Aboard one of the huge amphibious assault ships assigned to the Sixth Fleet carrier task force in the Mediterranean, Corporal Harvey Randall, helicopter mechanic, performs routine maintenance on one of the thirty troop-carrying helicopters aboard.

At the American Embassy in London, Corporal Steve Eder and Sergeant Bill Engeler check the credentials of visitors and give them directions to various offices.

THE UNITED STATES NAVY

The mission of the Navy is to be ready to fight to control the seas. That means both on the surface, under it, and in the air above.

To carry out this mission the Navy today has about 460 major ships, about 2500 small craft, almost 7000 aircraft, and a strength of a little over 500,000 men and women.

The major ships include 13 aircraft carriers, more than 150 major surface combat ships, over a hundred supply and support ships, and over a hundred submarines.

The ships are assigned to fleets. In the Atlantic and the Caribbean the Second Fleet patrols constantly. The Pacific east of Hawaii is assigned to the Third Fleet. The Mediterranean is the home of the Sixth Fleet, and the Seventh Fleet operates in the western Pacific and the Indian Ocean. A network of naval bases that stretches from Japan to Greece serves these fleets.

In time of peace the Navy often serves as an instrument of international relations. Naval vessels often make goodwill visits to friendly ports, and a warship or a task force cruising the waters off a trouble spot often prevents a crisis from flaring into a war.

A primary mission of all our armed forces is to deter other countries from attacking us by making it obvious to a potential enemy that even if he gets in the first blow we are capable of bouncing back and destroying him. Deterrence is the prevention of action by causing fear of the consequences. Undoubtedly one of the major weapons of deterrence is our nuclear-submarine fleet. A potential enemy can use satellites and spies to keep tabs on our air, land, and surface forces, but these submarines are hidden from enemy detection as they hover on station about two hundred feet below the surface of the oceans of the world. They are our invisible hands of strength, ready to reach out with missiles to strike any attacker.

Impact on Your Life-style

The sea dictates Navy life-style.

With the exception of a few schools, headquarters, and

naval air stations, all Navy bases are on or near the sea. If you join the Navy, the odds are you'll be stationed on the Atlantic, Pacific, or Gulf coast, or at an overseas base on such bodies of water as the Mediterranean or the Sea of Japan.

The other important thing to understand is that in the Navy you can expect to pull sea duty. Navy life is divided between sea duty and shore duty, with everything done ashore aimed at keeping the ships at sea combat-ready.

With the recent policy changes, even women can expect sea duty at some time in their careers.

"Sea duty" does not mean you'll spend all your time at sea. You'll be assigned to a ship, but your ship will have a "home port" and will spend about half its time in, or close to, that port. When your ship is at sea you'll find it makes frequent visits to other ports. Sea voyages are called cruises, but they aren't like cruising on an ocean liner. While at sea you'll be getting a lot of training that will mold you and your shipmates into a team that can handle any emergency.

Since a ship must be able to operate around the clock—it doesn't pull into a garage for the night—you will normally work a shift, or "watch." These shifts will give you regular hours, and you will have time off each day. You won't be able to run down to the base bowling alley or go downtown when you're off duty, so the Navy tries to provide both recreational and educational programs aboard ship. Depending on the size of the ship, there may be a library, electronic video games, college or technical classes, a gym, and even competitive sports programs like intership boxing.

Even on a submarine there's usually a place to get away from it all for at least a few minutes.

Most ships have closed-circuit TV, which is used to show training films to improve your skills as well as videotapes of regular TV shows and full-length movies. Space is tight, but adequate, and the old battleship-gray paint went out with the battleships. Ship interiors are now painted in cheerful colors, almost like a cruise liner.

One thing you can't do aboard ship that you can do in port—for better or worse—is reach in the refrigerator for a beer. Alcoholic drinks are not permitted aboard Navy ships. The days of the tot of grog are long gone. But you will always find plenty of soft drinks, milk, tea, and coffee, and on the larger ships there's usually even a soda fountain.

Since off-duty facilities are limited even on the largest ships, the Navy makes up for this by putting its recreation dollars into off-duty facilities in home ports. Most home ports provide everything from disco clubs to auto hobby shops for your use.

Shore duty in the Navy is about the same as base duty in the other services: regular hours, weekends off, and time to do your own thing. Since most naval bases are in port cities, you can usually live on base or find an apartment in the city. Even if you are on sea duty, you can usually live ashore while your ship is in port and come to work on the ship as if it were the building you work in.

There is a definite rotation program for sea/shore tours, but it depends on your rank, rating, and skill level, among other things, and is too involved to outline here. Personnel on an initial enlistment of four years or less can expect to be assigned to either sea or shore duty and stay on that type of duty for their entire tour.

A Moment in Time in the Navy

Off the coast of Florida, Petty Officer First Class Ron Gist, electrician's mate, monitors the test dials on the experimental 100-ton Surface Effect Ship as it whizzes over the waters of the Gulf of Mexico at close to 100 miles per hour.

At the Naval Air Station in Corpus Christi, Texas, on the other side of the Gulf, Petty Officer Third Class Janice Barber, aviation support equipment technician, is welding a break on a piece of ground-support equipment.

At San Diego, Petty Officer Third Class Duane Lincoln, data-processing technician, parks his motorcycle dockside and goes aboard his destroyer to put in a day's work getting her ready for her next patrol.

Aboard a nuclear-powered attack submarine submerged in the Pacific west of Hawaii and traveling at about thirty-five knots, Petty Officer Third Class Ray French, mess-management specialist, starts preparing breakfast for the crew.

At a submarine base in Scotland, Petty Officer Second Class Tony Rodriguez, torpedoman's mate, studies the wiring diagram of a new electronic torpedo system.

Somewhere in the North Atlantic, Lieutenant Junior Grade Warren Burack, combat-information-center watch officer, stands his watch on one of the destroyers taking part in a NATO antisubmarine warfare exercise.

SUMMARY

From this brief rundown you can see that your choice of service will have a lot to do with the life-style you'll be able to lead. Even though there is a similarity of jobs within the services, there is a vast difference in where you'll work and the conditions under which you'll work and live.

These differences should be considered when you make your choice of job and service.

CHAPTER FIVE

The Big
Red-White-and
Blue Schoolhouse

Just being in the armed forces is an education in itself, and, in addition, the services operate what is probably the largest school system in the world.

This system is designed to help you get both the education you need for your job and the education you want for your future, and includes on-duty career instruction, opportunities for college or vocational/technical schooling, and a program to help pay for your continuing education after you leave the service. There are even programs where you can learn hobbies or crafts just for the fun of it.

Educational opportunities are available in just about

any subject and on every level, and in most cases the military foots your bill, or at least a large part of it.

MILITARY SPECIALTY TRAINING

Most recruits have little civilian job experience, so they must be trained in a skill before they become productive. To provide this training, the services operate several hundred technical and specialty schools offering thousands of courses of instruction in hundreds of career fields. More than 300,000 military personnel graduate from these schools every year.

It would take many pages to list all the courses available, but just to indicate the variety, let's take a look at what's offered by the second-smallest service, the Marines, in the field of aviation. These are only basic courses.

Once you have attained a basic skill and shown an interest in staying in the Marines, you will be eligible for selection for advanced schooling. The Marines offer over 500 different skill courses, of which about 300 are advanced.

To put this in perspective, remember that the Marines are the second-smallest service, after the Coast Guard. The larger services, Air Force, Army, and Navy, offer both a larger variety and a greater number of skill courses.

What's Behind the Title?

Course titles really don't tell you much. What's important is whether a course will provide you with a marketa-

COURSE	LENGTH IN WEEKS	LOCATION
Air Controlman	13	Memphis, Tennessee
Air Support Operations	6	Twentynine Palms, California
Aviation Maintenance Administrative Clerk	7	Meridian, Mississippi
Aviation Machinist's Mate J (Jet engine) Course	7	Memphis, Tennessee
Aviation Machinist's Mate R (Reciprocating engine) Course	7	Memphis, Tennessee
Air Crew Survival Equipmentman	18	Lakehurst, New Jersey
Aviation Structure Mechanic E (Safety Equipment) Course	9	Memphis, Tennessee
Aviation Structure Mechanic H (Hydraulic) Course	7	Memphis, Tennessee
Aviation Structure Mechanic S (Structures) Course	8	Memphis, Tennessee
Cryogenics Equipment Technician	17	Portsmouth, Virginia
Aviation Support Equipment Technician, mechanical	9	Memphis, Tennessee
Aviation Support Equipment Technician, hydraulic	9	Memphis, Tennessee
Aviation Support Equipment Technician, electrical	12	Memphis, Tennessee

COURSE	LENGTH IN WEEKS	LOCATION
Basic Helicopter Course, Class C	6	Memphis, Tennessee
Aerial Navigator Course	22	Mather AFB, California
Airborne Radio Operator	16	Cherry Pt., North Carolina
Aviation Operations Clerical Course	7	Meridian, Mississippi
Aircraft Launch and Recovery Technician Course	7	Lakehurst, New Jersey
Aviation Crash, Fire and Rescueman	5	Memphis, Tennessee
Aviation Ordnanceman Course	13	Memphis, Tennessee
Aviation Repairman Course	20	Memphis, Tennessee
Aviation Repairman Course	10	Memphis, Tennessee
Avionics Technician Course	20	Memphis, Tennessee
Aviation Electrician's Mate	19	Memphis, Tennessee
Precision Measuring Technician	32	Lowry AFB, Colorado
Photography Mate Course	12	Pensacola, Florida
Marine Aviation Supply	10	Meridian, Mississippi
Aviation Radio Repairman	32	Twentynine Palms, California
Weather Observer/ Aerographer	15	Lakehurst, New Jersey

ble skill. To illustrate what you might expect to learn, let's take a brief look at one Army course. The description of it was taken directly from an Army publication, so don't feel bad if you don't understand all the terms.

Course: *Improved HAWK Mechanical Systems Repair*
Given at: U.S. Army Missile and Munitions Center and School, Redstone Arsenal, Alabama.

Purpose: To provide enlisted personnel with a working knowledge of inspecting, testing, and repairing the electrical, electromechanical, mechanical, hydraulic, and hydro-pneumatic portions of the Improved HAWK Missile System and associated test equipment.

Scope: Missile shop practices, principles of AC and AD circuits, hydraulic systems and pneumatic systems, Improved HAWK Weapon System Pulse Acquisition Radar, Range Only Radar, High Power Illuminator Radar, Continuous Wave Acquisition Radar, Launcher, Battery Control Central, Radar Signal Simulator, Information Coordination Central, hydraulic, electromechanical, pneumatic components, and associated test equipment. Inspection, testing, troubleshooting, and repair.

Prerequisites: Credit for a course in algebra and a background in general science, or have a standard score of 45 or higher in GED tests 3 and 5, high-school level. Twenty-one months or more active-duty service remaining after completion of the course. Standard score of 100 or higher in general maintenance-aptitude area. Be eligible to get a "Confidential" security clearance.

A lot of the above may read to you like a foreign language, but even without an interpreter, I'm sure you can see that if you graduate from a military-school course you'll have learned the rudiments of a marketable skill.

A word of explanation on that note about having 21 months or more of active duty left after you graduate. The services aren't spending a fortune to train you so you can get out and go to work as a civilian. You can do that eventually, of course, but to be able to get at least some use out of your expensive training, they all put limits on how late in your enlistment tour you can take a course. The more technical a course is and the longer it takes, the more time you'll have to have left after you finish it. So it pays to try to get into specialty courses as early in your enlistment as possible, or you may not make the cut-off.

Navy, Coast Guard, and Air Force Courses

In the Navy, basic job-entry-level skills are taught at approximately 80 schools. Entry-level courses are called Class A. The courses for entry-level skills vary from four weeks up to almost a year. This initial skill training gives you all the formal classroom training you'll need to make a rating at the lowest skill level. With Class A school training you are considered qualified to progress through on-the-job training from the apprentice to the journeyman level (E5–E6).

Once you have credit for an A school or have moved up the skill ladder through on-the-job training and correspondence courses, you become eligible for advanced training at a Class C school.

Let's say you are working on a rating of electrician's mate. Your training would probably go something like this. Immediately after boot camp you'd take a four to nine weeks course in basic electricity and electronics. This might be given at Orlando, Florida; San Diego, California; Chicago, Illinois; or Memphis, Tennessee. Then you would go to the electrician's mate Class A technical course at Great Lakes Naval Base near Chicago for another eight or nine weeks. Following this, you might be assigned directly to a job as an electrician's mate or you might be selected to go on to an advanced Class C school in a specialized electrical field such as minesweeping or repair of motion-picture equipment. Depending on the advanced specialty, a Class C course might be anywhere from one to a dozen weeks long.

If you were to receive training as a data systems technician you'd start off with the same basic electricity and electronics course as the electrician's mate, but then your follow-up would be a 26-week course in basic computer theory and maintenance at the Class A school in San Francisco. From there it would be either to a job or to a Class C school for an advanced specialty in the data-processing field.

The Coast Guard uses a similar method of lettered schools. Courses in the basic technical schools, the Class A schools, provide the training required to qualify you for advancement to petty officer third class (E-4). Because of the small size of the Coast Guard, personnel are often sent to the specialty schools of the other services for training, especially to Navy schools.

Opportunities for additional formal career training are available if you indicate that you are planning on the Coast Guard as a career. You could be sent to a Class B school, which is a school that gives you the knowledge you'll need to earn a rate higher than E-4, or a Class C school to provide you with specialized training in one aspect of your rating.

Approximately 90 percent of all Air Force recruits attend a technical school following basic training. The Air Force offers over 1500 career courses at five technical schools, a school of health-care sciences, and a school of applied cryptologic sciences. These schools graduate over 140,000 students a year.

All service schools use the most up-to-date teaching methods to ensure your success. The Air Force, for example, uses a job-relevant approach to career education, and with this technique of pitching the course to the needs of your job assignment can train a jet-engine mechanic in just eleven weeks. A mechanic so trained is capable of walking into a jet-engine repair shop and, with a minimum of supervision, beginning productive work immediately.

Training like this makes use of the most modern training aids, such as computers, which help the student progress at his or her own pace, while at the same time giving the instructors the freedom to provide assistance to individual students in a class.

Correspondence Courses

All the services provide some form of career training through correspondence courses. These courses are designed to let you increase your technical proficiency at your own pace and on your own time. Course material is furnished free. Normally a course consists of paperback books that keep you up-to-date in your skill and also help prepare you for advancement. Most include study references and periodic tests.

The Coast Guard and the Navy put particular emphasis on this self-study. The Commandant of the Coast Guard requires all enlisted personnel to attain a broad range of training in their jobs through the Coast Guard's correspondence-course program. The courses are often a requirement for promotion. If you don't complete the required courses, you don't advance.

What Does This Training Cost?

Naturally, the cost to the government of the training you receive varies widely, according to the length and complexity of the course you take. Using the Air Force as an example, the basic technical training course for a ground radio operator costs about $3,600. Training you to be an air control and warning radar repairman would cost about $15,000. And training you to be a pilot can run up to about $190,000.

You might be able to get training almost as good in a civilian school for less money, but then you'd have to pay your own living expenses while you went to school, plus the school bill itself. In the service they pay for the training as well as paying you.

In the long run, only you can determine how much this training is worth to you and whether it is money well spent. It's important to realize, however, that the services are willing to spend it on you.

CAREER TRAINING FOR OFFICERS

Education is a way of life for officers as well as enlisted personnel.

The career education pattern for officers in all services is approximately the same as that described below for a Marine officer.

The first school for all newly commissioned Marine second lieutenants is the Basic School at Quantico, Virginia. For twenty-one weeks you'll take courses in leadership, techniques of military instruction, marksmanship, map reading, communications, infantry tactics on the small unit level, infantry weapons and supporting arms, field engineering, Marine Corps organization and staff functions, drill, command and ceremonies, military law, logistics, company personnel administration, Marine Corps history and traditions, first aid, data-processing utilization, patrolling, combat operations, tank-infantry operations, aviation and air support, amphibious operations, contemporary operations, and physical training and conditioning techniques.

The next step will be a specialist school where you will learn all the details of your chosen occupational field. You might, for example, attend a three-month course to become a combat engineer, or a four-month course to become an air-control officer. Specialist courses last from six weeks to sixteen months and you may go to one right after basic training or any time during your first seven or eight years in the Corps. When you go depends on both the skill you want to learn and the Marines' need for you to learn it.

If you commit yourself to a career, the educational

program turns from strictly training to "professional" education. "Training" is classified as instruction aimed at giving you a technical skill or specialty. "Professional" education is aimed at the broader purpose of developing leaders and of giving you the big picture of how all the specialties fit together to carry out the service mission, and of how all this fits into military principles and concepts.

In your ninth year or so you will go to an intermediate-level school. This might be the Amphibious Warfare School or another Navy or Marine school, or perhaps even an Army school such as the Air Defense School at Fort Bliss, Texas.

Your schooling will continue as long as you are an officer in the service, even up to the rank of lieutenant colonel (O-5) and higher.

In addition, a large number of officers are given the opportunity to earn advanced degrees in civilian colleges and universities, and most officers take a number of short training courses at irregular intervals to prepare them for a special job or to keep them up-to-date.

OTHER EDUCATIONAL OPPORTUNITIES

In addition to the on-duty courses aimed at improving your expertise in your career specialty, all the services offer a wide variety of choices in voluntary, off-duty education programs that range from making up high school deficiencies to earning a Ph.D.

Almost every post or base has an education center that coordinates all the education programs available in the area. Even if no such center exists there will always be an education counselor available, either in person or by mail, to guide you. This may be an officer, an NCO, or a civilian educator who is knowledgeable enough to help you plan your education and work toward your goals as long as you are in the service.

A Problem Overcome

Travel is a major part of military life. Although this may be interesting in itself, it creates problems when you are trying to get a college degree or to earn a vocational or technical certificate. Too often a man or woman works hard to earn credits in one school, only to have the service transfer him or her to another place where the credits either aren't accepted or don't apply to the programs available at the school near the new duty station.

To overcome this problem, the Department of Defense and the various services have come up with a number of solutions.

Servicemen's Opportunity College

Each service is authorized to establish educational programs best suited to the needs of its own personnel. And to fill in the gaps and make certain you don't get shut out by your service's failings in this regard, the Department of Defense organized the Servicemen's Opportunity College (SOC).

SOC is a network of hundreds of junior, community, and four-year colleges that have agreed to help you pursue a coordinated program of study regardless of where you are stationed. As SOC members, the schools have agreed: (1) to have liberal entrance requirements; (2) to have liberal residency requirements adaptable to the mobility of military people; (3) to offer courses on base in the evenings, weekends, or any other time when it is most convenient to the class; (4) to provide special means for completing courses when they are interrupted by military requirements; (5) to provide tutorial assistance on request; (6) to designate a trained counselor for each student; (7) to grant credit for educational experiences gained in the service; and, (8) to have a transfer policy that is generous in its recognition of both traditional and nontraditional methods of education.

The Navy Campus for Achievement

The Navy's solution to the transfer problem is called the Navy Campus for Achievement (NCFA).

This is not a real campus, but rather an education management system that coordinates and records all the training you received in your pre-Navy days with the on-duty and off-duty educational credits you have earned while in the service, and provides you with advice and help. It makes it possible for you to obtain college degrees or professional certificates and diplomas by combining education, training, and work experience received in both civilian and military life.

A key part of NCFA is its network of professional advisers, who can, among other things, inform you of available off-duty educational opportunities, help you secure financial aid, when needed, advise you about the various schools that are available, and assist you, if you are qualified, in obtaining admission to full-time college programs such as the Naval Reserve Officer Training Corps and other two- and four-year college programs either totally or partially financed by the Navy.

Once you sign up with an NCFA-affiliated school you, the Navy, and the school enter into a partnership that will simplify the transfer of credits and pretty much eliminate residency requirements. Once accepted by an NCFA school, you usually have up to ten years to complete your degree or certification program.

Under the overall umbrella of NCFA there are also a number of specific educational programs. One of these is called PACE, which stands for Program for Afloat College Education. Under this program even the sailor at sea has the opportunity to take college courses. A half dozen colleges and universities conduct accredited courses for ships' crews. In many cases the courses are conducted by an instructor on board while the ship is at sea. When an instructor is not aboard, the sailor uses a study guide, complete with written assignments. PACE is available to all ships that can sign up at least ten members for each class. Ships as small as minesweepers, with an average crew of 45, have participated in PACE.

The courses offered are usually in the lower division of college, such as English, mathematics, economics, biology, sociology, and history. However, if enough students are available to form a class, upper-division courses are made available.

The extent of this program can be seen in the following statistics. In a recent year, one PACE contractor college conducted 550 college-level courses for 75 ships of the Pacific Fleet. At the same time another college contractor conducted 48 vocational courses for 16 ships, and a third conducted 80 courses on 22 ships. The heaviest users of the courses were aircraft carriers; as many as 41 courses were taught on them during the year.

Grades earned in this way become part of your NCFA record.

After you have been in the Navy awhile you might be eligible for other educational programs. Three programs offer qualified petty officers the opportunity for four years of college training and a commission. They are: the Navy Enlisted Scientific Education Program, the Navy Enlisted Dietetic Education Program, and the Navy Enlisted Nursing Education Program.

You will be made aware of the qualifications for these and for a number of other available educational programs after you are in the Navy.

Community College of the Air Force

The Air Force has its own recognized two-year college, based on Air Force skills. The Community College of the Air Force (CCAF) is a fully accredited educational institution offering an associate degree in applied science to enlisted men and women. Air Force technical education provides the base for CCAF programs. They can be rounded out later by civilian courses taken in off-duty time and by the completion of professional Air Force courses.

Each of the various study programs leading to an associate degree requires the completion of 64 semester hours of combined Air Force and civilian instruction. This includes 24 semester hours in technical education—all or part of which may be taken in Air Force schools—25 hours in general education, which is provided by regionally accredited civilian colleges and universities, and six hours of management education, which may be taken in either Air Force or civilian schools. The remaining nine mandatory hours are electives.

To get you started toward this degree, the CCAF is authorized to award you four semester hours of credit in physical education and first aid for the completion of your basic military training and additional hours for your work at a technical school after basic.

Up to 75 percent of the tuition for the civilian school courses will be paid for by the Air Force under the Tuition Assistance Program.

Associate-degree programs are divided into five specialty fields: aircraft and missile maintenance, electronics and telecommunications, health-care sciences, management and logistics, and public and support services. Under these five there are about 85 different majors you can pursue, and more are being added as fast as they can be developed and accredited. For example, under the field of management and logistics, you can get your degree in:

Administrative Assistant
Data Processing
Maintenance Production Management
Matériel Management
Procurement
Resource Management
Restaurant Management
Transpoı.ation and Traffic Management
Work-Center Management

The Air Force maintains a computerized student record of your progress. This record automatically picks up applicable Air Force instruction and translates it into semester hours in civilian educational terminology. You add your civilian courses by providing the appropriate documentation on them to the base education-services officer, who forwards them to the central computer station. You can get a copy of your transcript through the education officer at any time, anywhere in the world.

The Army's PROJECT AHEAD

In this world where every group tries to come up with a title that reads like a word, the Army stands near the front of the line. AHEAD stands for Army Help for Education And Development. This is another umbrella program covering all the Army's many educational opportunities. Under it you can pursue a college degree or get a vocational/technical education.

Project AHEAD makes it possible to start your educational program at the same time you enlist.

Here's the way it works. When you visit your Army recruiter, ask to see the "Project AHEAD" catalog. This gives information on the nearly 1400 colleges, universities, and vocational/technical schools participating in the program. It lists their requirements for admission and a summary of what academic programs they offer. You select the school or schools that interest you, and the recruiter will get you in touch with the adviser at that school who is appointed to counsel students in the program. The adviser will discuss the academic program you want and explain how you can take courses wherever you are stationed and tell you how to earn credit for regular Army training and experience. When you find the school that fits your needs and plans, you sign up for AHEAD at the same time you enlist. The school of your choice becomes your "home" school, no matter where it is located.

When you are in the Army you coordinate with your home school through the counselor at the post education center. Your home school adviser will tell you which of the courses available through the education center will be accepted in your program.

With a three-year enlistment it is possible to earn a substantial number of credits that will be accepted by your home school when you get out of the service. Credits can be earned from a variety of sources, including service schools (basic combat training, advanced individual training), correspondence courses, and courses taken at other civilian schools.

SOME OTHER PROGRAMS

Along with the Servicemen's Opportunity College, the Navy Campus for Achievement, the Community College of the Air Force, and Project AHEAD, there are a number of other ways you can get the education you want.

Tuition Assistance

Uncle Sam will pick up as much as 75 percent of the tab for any approved courses you take in civilian schools while you are on active duty. In the Coast Guard, because it is not under Department of Defense restrictions, you may be able to get your courses completely paid for.

What is an approved course? Almost anything that grants school credit. You will have to apply for this assistance through the education center, and the advisers there will tell you if the course is approved or not.

Degree-Completion Programs

If you are already well along on your associate or bachelor's degree, all the services have programs where you may apply to go to school full time to finish that degree. This means full time while you still draw your active-duty pay and allowances. In such cases, since you are being paid while you go to school, you will have to pay your own school bills.

There is a lot of competition to get in these programs, and they are normally only available to officers and NCOs. However, in some cases, such as when you are working toward a degree that the service needs, you will be eligible even if you are in a lower rank. Some of these programs lead to commissions. All require signing up for additional service.

Advanced-Degree Programs

Exceptional officers may apply to or be selected to go to school full time to earn an advanced degree (master's or doctorate) in a field that is needed by their particular service. If you apply for this and are accepted, you will stay on active duty with full pay and allowances, but will have to pay your own school bills. If you are selected and ordered to a school, then the military pays your school bills. One reason for selection is to train an officer to become an instructor at one of the military academies. Naturally, these programs are aimed at careerists.

CLEP

In this case the letters stand for the College Level Examination Program. This is a program run by civilian colleges of which the military can take advantage. It lets you complete selected college courses by examination only. In other words, if you know a subject but don't have actual classroom credit for it, you can earn that credit by examination. Let's say your high school had an exceptional English department and by the time you graduated you had finished the equivalent of what a freshman would take in college. Rather than force you to take freshman English, and be bored, the college offers you the opportunity to test out of it. If you pass the CLEP test, you get credit for the course and can go on to take other, more interesting and more advanced courses.

You can take up to 30 semester hours of freshman-level college credit in this way. General exams are given in English, social science, natural science, the humanities, and mathematics. Besides these general exams there are a number of subject exams you can take, such as languages.

The program is free and the base education centers maintain a list of the current college courses that you can get credit for through CLEP.

Military Colleges

The Air Force Institute of Technology at Wright-Patterson AFB, in Ohio, and the Naval Postgraduate School in Monterey, California, are two degree-granting military schools. The Air Force Institute offers both undergraduate and advanced degrees in logistics and specialized Air Force engineering areas. The Naval Postgraduate School offers advanced degrees primarily in the scientific and engineering areas.

With few exceptions, these schools are only for officers.

Correspondence Courses

Through the education centers you can enroll in any one of hundreds of correspondence courses from both civilian and military sources. Most of these courses are either free or low cost, and they include career development, general knowledge, and fun courses. The Air Force, for example, has the Extension Course Institute, which offers nearly 400 courses. Some 250,000 Air Force personnel enroll in these courses annually.

Fun Courses

If you want to learn karate, candlemaking, hang gliding, private flying, or gourmet cooking, you will probably find a course in it offered through the education center, the Service or Enlisted Club, or various groups on the base. These noncredit courses are often developed to meet the request of a group of service personnel who share a common interest. Therefore, if what you want isn't available, ask for it, and someone will try to fill your need.

PUTTING IT ALL TOGETHER

The term "education center" or "education services center" has popped up a number of times so far. No matter what name the different services pin on it, this is the place on each base or post where you can get both counseling and courses to advance your education. A typical Army center is the Fort Knox Education Center at Fort Knox, Kentucky, which provides all the assistance you need to take part in all the DOD and Army programs described above. It also offers a number of courses and programs on the post.

There will undoubtedly be a number of changes by the time you read this, but the following shows what was available there in 1979, and it's a good example of what you can expect to find on any major base. At Fort Knox the cooperating colleges and universities providing educational opportunities are:

> University of Kentucky Center at Fort Knox
> Western Kentucky University
> Eastern Kentucky University
> University of Southern California
> The Embry-Riddle Aeronautical University
> Elizabethtown Community College

High-school refresher/college-preparatory courses are also offered. The Elizabethtown Community College, University of Kentucky at Fort Knox, offers a six-week on-duty educational program that leads to a high-school equivalency diploma, remedial or refresher courses preparatory to college entrance, and educational skill courses necessary for advancement in the military or for civilian employment. All servicemen with more than 180 days of consecutive military service are eligible.

Western Kentucky University is offering an extended campus in-residence program that may be used to satisfy a professional education requirement for the vocational-technical and industrial A.S. and B.S. teaching degree of a Kentucky Trades and Industries Certificate. A typical program leading to a certificate or A.S. degree would include: vocational-industrial and technical teachers education, industrial electrical technology, drafting and design, power-mechanic technology, building-construction technology, and small-business management.

The offerings of several universities have been coordinated at Fort Knox to provide programs for the person motivated toward career-oriented programs in retail management, business management, real estate, law enforcement, aviation maintenance technology, and other vocational-industrial and technical teacher education areas.

In addition, all courses taken on the post count as resident credit in meeting the degree requirements of the different universities. Here are some typical academic offerings:

Engineering Drafting
Basic Woodwork
Basic Metalwork
Basic Electricity

Basic Electronics
Advanced Engineering Drafting
Auto Mechanics
Principles of Accounting I
Principles of Accounting II
Human Ancestry
Principles of Plant Biology
Principles of Economics I
Principles of Economics II
Human Development
Principles of College Composition
Freshman Composition I
Advanced Freshman Composition
Western Literature
Modern Social Problems
Basic German I
Basic German II
Intermediate German
Business Management
Analysis of Organizational Behavior
Business Law
Urban Geography
Seminar in National Government
Seminar in Public Affairs
Group Guidance
Counseling Practicum
Industrial Wood Processing
Advanced Auto Mechanics
Beginning Shorthand
Essentials of Real Estate
Real Estate Marketing
Retail Management
Basic Photography
History of Europe 1713 to Present

History of US through 1865
College Algebra
Fundamental Concepts of Math I
Introduction to Music
Introduction to Physics
American Government
Introduction to Political Behavior
World Politics
Psychological Differences
General Psychology
Basic Public Speaking
Introduction to Social Sciences
Economic Theories
Personal and Community Health
Educational Tests and Measurement
Court Procedures and Mechanics
Police Administration
Laws of Search, Arrest, and Seizure
Fundamentals of Reading Instruction
Introduction to Guidance
Educational Foundations

And remember, this is just an example.

AND AFTER YOU GET OUT

So far we've covered the educational opportunities you'll have in the service. But what about paying the bill when you get out?

Under the new Veterans' Educational Assistance Program, Uncle Sam will add two dollars to every one dollar you put into an education fund while you're in the service. The maximum under the VEAP is $8100, but your share of that will be just $2700, whereas the government puts in $5400.

The rules are simple. You may choose to save between the minimum of $50 a month and the maximum of $75 in $5 increments. Here's how that would stack up for $50, $60, or $75 a month.

YOU SAVE PER MONTH	YOUR TOTAL	UNCLE SAM'S SHARE	TOTAL
	after one year		
$50	$600	$1200	$1800
$60	720	1440	2160
$75	900	1800	2700
	after two years		
$50	$1200	$2400	$3600
$60	1440	2880	4320
$75	1800	3600	5400
	after three years		
$50	$1800	$3600	$5400
$60	2160	4320	6480
$75	2700	5400	8100

The second rule is that the money in the fund can be used only for school. You can't use Uncle Sam's share to buy a car or put a down payment on a house. And the school must be an accredited college or vocational/ technical school.

You will be paid a monthly installment of the total as long as you are actively enrolled in school, or until the money runs out.

Looking at the high cost of college these days, even $8100 won't buy many years in school. But couple that with all the education you can get while you are in the service and that VEAP package will probably be enough to see you through to a degree. In addition, the Army gives educational bonuses of up to $6000 if you enlist for four years in certain specialties.

If you don't go to school, you'll get back all the money you put in but not a dollar of Uncle Sam's.

If $50 or $75 a month sounds like a big bite, remember that your base pay alone at the lowest enlisted grade is well over $400 a month. So if you are serious about completing your education, you'll have the money to save for it. It's a matter of putting your money where it will do you the most good in the long run.

SUMMARY

It's interesting to note that in a number of surveys the statistics have shown that military veterans are better educated, better paid, and there is less unemployment among them than nonveterans. And those surveys were taken before all the educational programs outlined here were in existence.

Although this chapter is crammed with details on the various programs, it was not meant to overwhelm you, but rather to give you a solid idea of the wealth of choices for an education you can find in the service if you want to take advantage of it.

Like everything else in the service, educational programs come and go and change, so some of the programs listed here might not be in effect when you join, but you can be sure there will be others similar to them. The services are committed to helping you get an education, not only to keep you happier as a serviceman, but also for their own benefit, because they know that knowledge is power and that a knowledgeable serviceman adds power to their service.

Overall, it's easy to see that if you want to use the service to further your education, you can do it. It's up to you.

CHAPTER SIX

Training for a Civilian Career

So far we have discussed pay and benefits, life-styles and schools. Now let's get down to the theme of this book: how to start a civilian career in the military. That means talking about jobs.

Even if you definitely would not consider a lifetime career in the military, you should give serious thought to the idea of using the outstanding free training the services offer as a means to prepare yourself for a rewarding civilian career. As an employer, the military services offer you a choice of jobs and training unmatched by even the largest civilian firms. And, as noted before, many of these jobs are similar to those you would hold as a civilian.

To understand why there are so many civilian-type jobs

in the military, you must first understand that the services are organized to be self-sufficient in a crisis. That means each one must have trained personnel with all the basic skills and trades necessary to carry on the daily business of living as if it were a small, isolated community. The butcher, baker, policeman, fireman, water-supply operator, secretary, doctor, lawyer, plumber, electrician, carpenter—they are all essential.

To make this more clear, I have prepared a list of over one hundred civilian jobs that are duplicated in all five services, with almost exactly the same duties as in the civilian job. Sometimes the work done in the military job is much broader than in the civilian job, in which case the title is different. For example, the civilian title diesel mechanic doesn't cover all the work of an Air Force general-purpose-vehicle repairman, who works on both diesel and internal-combustion engines and may also service front-end and steering systems.

Civilian Jobs That Are Available in the Military

Accounting Clerk
Aircraft Engine Mechanic
Aircraft Inspector
Aircraft Load Control Agent
Aircraft Mechanic (plumbing and hydraulics)
Air-Traffic Controller
Announcer
Auditor
Automobile Mechanic

Baker
Bookkeeper
Bricklayer
Bulldozer Operator
Cable Splicer
Camera Operator
Camera Repairer
Canvas Worker
Carpenter
Cement Mason
Chemical Operator
Clerk-typist
Commercial Photographer
Computer Operator
Computer Programmer
Construction Equipment Mechanic
Construction Worker
Cook
Court Reporter
Cryptographic Machine Operator
Detective
Photo Developer
Diesel Mechanic
Diesel Plant Operator
Disaster/Damage Control Specialist
Diver
Draftsman
Driller, Water-Well
Film Editor
Electrical-Instrument Repairer
Electrician
Electrician, Airplane
Electrician, Automotive
Electrician, Powerhouse

Electronics Mechanic
Electronics Technician
Engineering Equipment Mechanic
Fire-Control-Instrument Repairer
Fire Fighter
Fire Marshal
Food and Drug Inspector
Fuel Pumper
Guard
Gunsmith
Illustrator/Commercial Artist
Instrument Mechanic
Intelligence Clerk
Key-Punch Operator
Law Clerk
Legal Secretary
Machinist
Marksmanship Instructor
Metallurgist
Meteorologist
Missile Mechanic
Munitions Assembler
Musician
Office Manager
Ordnance Artificer
Painter, Aircraft
Painter, Rough
Parachute Rigger
Payroll Clerk
Plumber
Police Officer
Power Plant Operator
Power Shovel Operator
Producer

Radar Operator
Radio Mechanic
Radio Operator
Refrigeration Mechanic
Reporter
Rigger
Sheet-Metal Worker
Shipping Clerk
Secretary
Stock-Control Clerk
Structural Steel Worker
Surveyor
Switchboard Operator
Tabulating Machine Operator
Telephone Installer/Repairer
Television Service and Repairer
Traffic Manager
Transmission Mechanic
Travel Clerk
Truck Driver, Heavy
Truck Driver, Light
Truck Driver, Tractor-Trailer
Water Treatment Plant Operator
Weather Observer
Welder
Wire Lineman

That should be enough to give you an idea of what is available. And it's only part of the list.

Lists are good starters, good ways to narrow down your choices. But once you've narrowed down to what you think might interest you, you need more details. Once again, it would take an encyclopedia to give details on all the jobs that are civilian related, so all I can do is give you a sample. The forty jobs that follow were selected because they are jobs you should recognize and understand from their titles alone.

Some of these jobs, such as an electronics repairman, are difficult to get because the qualifications are high. Some require special talent and prior training, such as for musician. But most of them are jobs you can qualify for with just a high-school education and average abilities, and you'll find it easier to break into many of them in the military than in civilian life. For example, have you tried to become a plumber lately?

Since officer careers are often directly related to the individual's college background in fields like accounting, law, and medicine, this sample is restricted to jobs available to enlisted personnel only.

DETAILS ON FORTY CIVILIAN-TYPE JOBS

As you look over the selection that follows, there are a few things you should note. First of all, the job descriptions have been simplified. All kinds of "ifs, buts, and therefores" go with each job, but the same thing happens when you are job hunting in the civilian world, so they have been left out. If you are interested in a particular job, you'll be able to find out all the details from the recruiter.

In many cases you'll find that the civilian and military jobs are almost identical. Where there is a difference, you will find that the military job is wider in scope. A job that may require only one skill in civilian life may require many related skills in the military, which means you will be trained in all those skills, not just one. Each service usually has its own list of special qualifications for each job, so once again, check with your recruiter.

In 1979, not all the jobs were open to women, but most of the restrictions are in the process of being lifted.

All the civilian jobs chosen for this sample have a comparable military job in at least three services—most in all five services—so if you find the job you like here, you will have a wide choice of services in which to try for it. The civilian job titles are given at the head of each section.

Air Conditioning/Refrigeration Mechanic

General Civilian Job Information: As an air conditioning/refrigeration mechanic you must be a jack of many trades to be able to work on units ranging in size from simple home window units to large commercial central plant systems. To install, service, and repair this equipment may require you to weld or solder and, at times, be both a pipefitter and electrician. Entry into this craft is difficult and is normally through an on-the-job apprenticeship program that could last up to six years.

General Military Job Information: You will install, modify, and repair refrigeration, air-conditioning, and ventilation equipment of all types. This will include installing mechanical, pneumatic, electronic and sensing/switching devices designed to control flow and temperature of air, refrigerants, or working fluids. You will connect wiring harnesses to electrical equipment, and you will shape, size, and connect tubing to components such as meters, gauges, traps, and filtering assemblies using special bending, flaring, and coupling tools and oxyacetylene torches for soldering and brazing. You will also conduct tests of installed equipment. All the services have school training courses available to qualified personnel for entry into this specialty.

What are the basic qualifications for the job? Mechanical aptitude including good eye-hand coordination and finger and hand control are needed to use standard and hand power-operated tools accurately and safely . . . ability to learn to use drawings and blueprints . . . normal color vision . . . ability to use basic shop mathematics.

Helpful High-School Courses or Experience: Mechanical and electrical shops, basic mathematics, physics, and chemistry. Experience in metalwork, welding, electronics or machine repair very helpful.

Open to Women in: Air Force, Army, Marine Corps, Navy.

Equivalent Military Job:

Air Force	Refrigeration and Air-Conditioning Specialist
Army	Heating and Cooling Specialist
Coast Guard	Machinery Technician. (This is a much broader job classification. In addition to refrigeration work you will operate, maintain, and repair internal-combustion engines, propulsion boilers, steam turbines, and power-transmission equipment.)
Marine Corps	Refrigeration Mechanic
Navy	Refrigeration and Air-Conditioning Mechanic

Aircraft Engine Mechanic

General Civilian Job Information: There are many specialties within this career field, such as jet or propellor (reciprocating-engine) mechanic and helicopter mechanic. But in general, as an aircraft mechanic you will have to inspect, adjust, repair, and replace engine components, perform operational checks, perform routine maintenance, and prepare aircraft for flight. You also will normally be required to keep records. Entry into this specialty is difficult and usually requires a long period of on-the-job apprenticeship training and/or costly specialized schooling. (Ex-military mechanics are a prime source for filling civilian job vacancies.)

General Military Job Information: Normally your duties as an aircraft engine mechanic in the military will be the same as in a civilian job. All services have school courses available to qualified personnel for entry into this field.

What are the basic qualifications for the job? You will need a high degree of mechanical aptitude including eye-hand coordination and ability to use tools . . . above average ability to learn to read and understand technical instructions . . . ability to keep accurate records . . . normal color vision . . . physical strength.

Helpful High-School Courses or Experience: Mechanical and electrical shops, basic mathematics, physics. Work experience in engine repair or a sheet-metal shop will be especially helpful.

Open to Women in: Air Force, Army, Coast Guard, Marine Corps, Navy.

Equivalent Military Jobs:

Air Force   Jet-Engine Mechanic, Reciprocating Engine Mechanic, Helicopter Mechanic

Army	Airplane Repairman, Helicopter Repairman, Aircraft Turbine Engine Repairman
Coast Guard	Aviation Machinist's Mate
Marine Corps	Aircraft Power Plant Mechanic, Helicopter Mechanic, Aircraft Mechanic/Reciprocating
Navy	Aviation Machinist's Mate

Air Traffic Controller (Tower)

General Civilian Job Information: As an air-traffic controller in an airport tower you will supervise flight operations within a specific area and issue orders to pilots. You will determine each plane's altitude, inform pilots about weather, wind direction, other aircraft, and proper approaches and runways for taxiing, take-offs, and landings. You will also maintain contact with air-traffic control centers that coordinate the movement of aircraft out of the range of your control. Entry into this position is very difficult and usually requires some type of related experience. Those accepted for training attend the Federal Aviation Administration's school to qualify to be an assistant controller. It normally takes a minimum of two years on-the-job training to qualify as a certified controller.

General Military Job Information: As a military air-traffic controller your duties will be about the same as in a civilian job. Opportunities in this specialty are limited to highly qualified personnel. All services provide basic schooling for those selected, which normally leads to FAA certification.

What are the basic qualifications for this job? You must

be physically and emotionally able to operate with a high degree of precision, self-reliance, and calmness under stress . . . have a clear speaking voice and excellent vision and hearing . . . good mechanical and reasoning aptitudes.

Helpful High-School Courses or Experience: English, public speaking, mathematics, physics, and electrical shop. Experience in radio broadcasting might be helpful.

Open to Women in: Air Force, Army, Coast Guard, Marine Corps, Navy.

Equivalent Military Job:

Air Force	Air-Traffic Controller
Army	Air-Traffic Control Tower Operator
Coast Guard	Air Controlman
Marine Corps	Air-Traffic Controller—Tower Operator
Navy	Air Controlman

Automobile Body Repairman

General Civilian Job Information: As an automobile body repairman you will repair damaged automobile and light truck bodies and body parts. This normally includes removing damaged fenders, panels, grilles, or other parts, using power tools and welding equipment, preparing surfaces for refinishing by sanding or grinding, and repainting the repaired part. Entry into this specialty is normally through on-the-job training in an assistant's position.

General Military Job Information: Your duties in this job in the military will be basically the same as in a civilian repairshop. In some services, however, automotive body repair is only part of a larger job. Entry into this field may be through school training or on-the-job training.

What are the basic qualifications for the job? You should have good mechanical aptitude . . . the ability to do detailed work . . . normal color vision . . . and physical strength.

Helpful High-School Courses or Experience: Metal or machine shop, automobile mechanics, mechanical drawing. Experience in a garage, body repair shop, or sheet-metal shop will be very helpful.

Open to Women in: Air Force, Army, Marine Corps, Navy.

Equivalent Military Job:

Air Force	Vehicle Body Repairman
Army	Metal Body Repairman
Marine Corps	Body Repairman
Navy	Construction Mechanic. (Body repair is only one part of the duties of this job. The construction mechanic does repair work and maintenance on heavy construction and automotive equipment up to a major overhaul.)

Automobile Mechanic

General Civilian Job Information: As an automobile mechanic you will inspect, maintain, and repair internal-combustion-engine vehicles. This may include determining malfunctions by using test equipment, and repairing any of the various systems, such as mechanical, electrical, brakes, steering, or suspension. Entry into this field is usually easy and most training is on the job.

General Military Job Information: As an automobile mechanic in the military your duties will be similar to those in a civilian shop, but the variety of vehicles may be greater and there will be a wider range of specialties you can concentrate on. Entry into this field usually requires attendance at a basic mechanics course but may be accomplished by on-the-job training.

What are the basic qualifications for this job? You will need good mechanical aptitude, especially in eye-hand coordination and ability to work with tools . . . normal color vision . . . ability to learn to read technical manuals.

Helpful High-School Courses or Experience: Electrical and automotive shop, physics, basic mathematics, mechanical drawing. Any work or hobby experience working on motors will be helpful.

Open to Women in: Air Force, Army, Coast Guard, Marine Corps, Navy.

Equivalent Military Job:

Air Force	General-Purpose-Vehicle Repairman
Army	Automotive Repairman
Coast Guard	Machinery Technician. (This is a much broader job classification. In addition to automotive repair you will operate, maintain, and repair all types of internal-combustion engines, propulsion boilers, steam turbines, and power-transmission equipment.)
Marine Corps	Organizational Automotive Mechanic

Navy   Construction Mechanic. (This is
                                  also a broader job classification
                                  because you may also work on
                                  diesel engines and do body repair.)

Aviation Electrician

General Civilian Job Information: As an aviation
electrician you will install, inspect, adjust, repair, and
maintain a variety of electrical systems in aircraft. These
may include power generators, compasses, lighting systems, fuel-indicating systems, and automatic flight-
control systems, among others. You will normally perform
both preflight and postflight checks. Entry into this field is
difficult and normally requires a long period of on-the-job
apprenticeship training and/or costly special schooling.

General Military Job Information: Normally your duties
as an aviation electrician in the military will be the same
as in the civilian job, but you may also work on more
advanced systems that have not yet been adopted by
civilian aircraft owners.

What are the basic qualifications for this job? You will
need a high degree of mechanical aptitude . . . good
vision, including normal color vision and night vision . . .
the ability to keep accurate records . . . the ability to do
precise work when performing detailed or repetitive
tasks . . . the ability to reason systematically when doing
troubleshooting.

Helpful High-School Courses or Experience: Electrical
or electronics shops, algebra, trigonometry, and physics.
Work experience with electrical or electronic systems,
especially aircraft or automotive, are especially helpful.

Open to Women in: Air Force, Army, Coast Guard,
Marine Corps, Navy.

Equivalent Military Job:

Air Force	Aircraft Electrical Repairman
Army	Avionics Mechanic
Coast Guard	Aviation Electrician's Mate
Marine Corps	Aircraft Electrician
Navy	Aviation Electrician's Mate

Bookkeeper

General Civilian Job Information: As a bookkeeper you will keep systematic records and up-to-date accounts of the financial transactions of a business or industrial firm. You will keep records on what the business owns and owes as well as of the profit and loss from its operations. In a small business you will probably keep the complete financial records, usually by hand with an adding machine. In a large firm you will probably be in a specialized department, such as payroll or taxes, and use more complicated bookkeeping machines. Entry into this field is fairly easy if you show an aptitude. It usually requires some high-school or business-school training, followed by on-the-job training.

General Military Job Information: As a bookkeeper in the military you will normally be doing the same kind of work as in a large firm. There are school courses available for those qualified to enter the field.

What are the basic qualifications for the job? You must have ability in basic mathematics . . . be able to work systematically with close attention to detail . . . have good eye-hand coordination . . . neatness . . . and good eyesight (with or without corrective glasses).

Helpful High-School Courses or Experience: Bookkeeping, general business, typing, vocational office education, statistics. Any office-work experience will be helpful.

Open to Women in: Air Force, Army, Coast Guard, Marine Corps, Navy.

Equivalent Military Job:

Air Force	General Accounting Specialist
Army	Finance Specialist
Coast Guard	Storekeeper. (This job classification is broader than just bookkeeping and includes providing and accounting for pay, clothing, commissary items, and spare parts.)
Marine Corps	Bookkeeper
Navy	Disbursing Clerk

Carpenter

General Civilian Job Information: As a carpenter you will work with wood doing either "rough" or "finish" work. "Rough" carpentry includes framing, boarding, and the installation of subflooring and other wood structures that will not be seen in the finished job. "Finish" carpentry includes finishing flooring, doors, siding, and other wood structures, which will be seen in the completed job. Normally entry into this job is through an apprenticeship program, which may last about four years. (One of the hazards of this job, as with all construction work, is that layoffs due to construction slowdowns can be expected.)

Military Job Information: In most of the services you will do carpentry as just one part of a larger construction specialty. Entry into this field is not difficult for those qualified and usually includes a basic school course and on-the-job training.

What are the basic qualifications for this job? You must have good mechanical abilities, especially eye-hand coordination . . . the ability to learn to read blueprints and technical drawings . . . a knowledge of basic arithmetic . . . and the ability to work in high places.

Helpful High-School Courses or Experience: Basic mathematics, woodworking shop, drafting. Any work experience in the building trades or woodworking would be very helpful.

Open to Women in: Air Force, Army, Navy.

Equivalent Military Job:

Air Force	Carpentry Specialist
Army	Carpenter
Coast Guard	Damage Controlman. (As a damage controlman, carpentry may be just one of your duties. You will be responsible for the preservation of modern safety and survival devices aboard ship, which may require you to do welding, firefighting, and pipefitting as well as woodworking.)
Marine Corps	Combat Engineer. (This is also a much broader job classification. As a combat engineer you may be called on to build and repair buildings, use rigging devices to move heavy objects, and help with destroying road blocks, bridges, and roads.)
Navy	Builder. (Another broad job classification under which you may work as a carpenter, plasterer, roofer, or heavy-equipment operator, or in various other construction trades.)

Clerk-Typist

General Civilian Job Information: As a clerk-typist your main work will be typing, but you will have other clerical duties, which may include filing and operating office machines. Entry into this field is not difficult if you have had high-school training in typing and office work. Most training is on the job.

General Military Job Information: Your job as a clerk-typist in the military will be about the same as in a civilian business. Entry into this field is usually based on typing ability developed in high-school or business-school courses, but basic courses in military administration are available to qualified personnel.

What are the basic qualifications for this job? You should be able to type—normally at least 30 words a minute . . . be able to do detailed and repetitive work accurately . . . be able to read and understand written instructions and to follow established procedures carefully.

Helpful High-School Courses or Experience: Typing, business-machine operation, business mathematics, English. Any work experience in an office that involved typing and filing will be valuable.

Open to Women in: Air Force, Army, Coast Guard, Marine Corps, Navy.

Equivalent Military Job:

Air Force	Administration Specialist. (This is a much broader job classification. As an administration specialist you may perform all types of administrative functions as well as typing and filing.)
Army	Clerk-Typist

Coast Guard	Yeoman. (This is another classification which is much broader than just clerk-typist. As yeoman you will perform a wide variety of administrative functions to prepare, record, and keep the vast amount of letters, messages, and reports flowing smoothly.)
Marine Corps	Administrative Clerk
Navy	Yeoman. (This is also a broader job classification. As a yeoman you will do all types of secretarial and clerical work.)

Commercial Photographer

General Civilian Job Information: As a commercial photographer you must be able to use a variety of camera lenses and accessories to produce a desired photo for a customer or client, and you must be able to develop, enlarge, and print pictures. Entry into this field usually requires some specialized training after high school or service as an apprentice with on-the-job training.

General Military Job Information: In the military your duties as a photographer will be about the same as in a civilian job. Some basic school courses are available to selected personnel, but most training in on the job.

What are the basic qualifications for this job? You should have a feeling for what is pleasing to the eye and composition . . . a creative imagination . . . good eye-hand coordination . . . the ability to get along well with people . . . the ability to produce under pressure . . normal color vision.

Helpful High-School Courses or Experience: Physics, chemistry, photography, art. Any work experience in photography or art will be helpful.

Open to Women in: Air Force, Army, Coast Guard, Marine Corps, Navy.

Equivalent Military Job:

Air Force	Still Photographic Specialist
Army	Still Photographer
Coast Guard	Photo-Journalist. (This is a broader job classification. As a photojournalist you will be a writer/reporter as well as a photographer. You may take both still and motion picture footage.)
Marine Corps	Photographer
Navy	Photographer's Mate. (This is also a broader job classification because the photographer's mate may be assigned duties with both still and motion-picture cameras.)

Computer Equipment Operator

General Civilian Job Information: As a computer equipment operator you may operate either the computer itself or associated equipment. You set up the program to be used, the work tapes or data cards, connect auxiliary equipment, and operate the computer console. Entry into this field is difficult because most employers require some training in data-processing technology before hiring. This may require some college or junior college training or training in an expensive data-processing school.

General Military Job Information: In the military the

job of a computer equipment operator is generally the same as that in a civilian firm. Entry into this specialty is difficult unless you are highly qualified, but selected basic school courses are provided before on-the-job training.
What are the basic qualifications for this job? You must have mechanical skill . . . be able to reason well . . . be willing to follow instructions precisely . . . have good reading skills and be able to pay close attention to details . . . have excellent eye-hand coordination . . . work well with numbers.

Helpful High-School Courses or Experience: Typing, business courses, English, mathematics including algebra, electronics. Any work experience using office machines or data-processing equipment would be helpful.

Open to Women in: Air Force, Army, Coast Guard, Marine Corps, Navy.

Equivalent Military Job:

Air Force	Computer Operator
Army	Computer Systems Operator
Coast Guard	Computer Console Operator
Marine Corps	Computer Operator
Navy	Data-Processing Technician

Computer Programmer

General Civilian Job Information: As a computer programmer you will analyze the steps the computer must go through to solve a problem and put the procedure into a coded form that the computer can follow. You will prepare the charts or instructions the computer console operator will follow, and follow up to see that the program works and has produced the desired result. Entry into this field is difficult and often comes from promotion from within the personnel already working in computer operations. Most employers require some junior college training in the field.

General Military Job Information: In the military the fundamentals of your job as a computer programmer will be the same as in a civilian firm. Entry into the field is restricted to highly qualified personnel, but the services provide basic schooling for those selected before on-the-job training.

What are the basic qualifications for this job? You must have an aptitude for logical thinking . . . be patient and persistent . . . be able to analyze a problem or a system and translate the heart of it into computer language . . . have strong mathematical ability, the ability to do detailed work with great accuracy, and the ability to learn to read technical publications.

Helpful High-School Courses or Experience: English, algebra, geometry, data processing and computer sciences. Any work experience in data processing will be helpful.

Open to Women in: Air Force, Army, Coast Guard, Marine Corps, Navy.

Equivalent Military Job:

Air Force	Programming Specialist
Army	Computer Programmer
Coast Guard	Computer Programmer
Marine Corps	Programmer
Navy	Computer Programmer

Construction Equipment Operator

General Civilian Job Information: As a construction equipment operator, sometimes called an operating engineer, you will operate heavy construction machinery such as bulldozers, pile drivers, power shovels, rollers, graders, and the like. Your exact title will often be identified with the machine you operate. Entry into this field is normally by on-the-job training or as part of an apprenticeship program. Entry is difficult.

General Military Job Information: In the military your job as a construction equipment operator will be about the same as on a civilian construction site. Entry into this field is limited to highly qualified personnel. Basic school courses are offered before on-the-job training.

What are the basic qualifications for this job? You must have a mechanical aptitude including excellent coordination of eye-hand-foot movements . . . physical strength . . . the ability to do repetitive tasks.

Helpful High-School Courses or Experience: Mechanical shop, arithmetic, drafting, automotive and electrical shop. Any experience in construction and automotive repair would be valuable.

Open to Women in: Air Force, Army, Coast Guard, Marine Corps, Navy.

Equivalent Military Job:

Air Force	Construction Equipment Operator
Army	General Construction Machine Operator
Coast Guard	Equipment Operator
Marine Corps	Engineer Equipment Operator
Navy	Equipment Operator

Construction Worker

General Civilian Job Information: As a construction worker you may load, unload, and move building materials to and from trucks; mix, pour, and spread concrete, asphalt, gravel, or other materials; use hand tools for rough labor. This is usually considered an unskilled job, but some laborers do jobs that require a considerable amount of know-how. Entry into the field is not difficult if you are in good physical condition. Training is on the job.

General Military Job Information: Although some of the military jobs in construction are laborer jobs, most require some additional skills. Entry into this field is not difficult if you are in good physical condition. Initial training is usually in basic school courses followed by on-the-job training.

What are the basic qualifications for this job? You must have mechanical aptitude, good physical endurance, and the ability to work under adverse conditions.

Helpful High-School Courses or Experience: No special training is required for initial employment, but for advancement it would be helpful to have had courses in mechanical drawing, construction work or other shops, basic mathematics. Work experience in construction would be helpful.

Open to Women in: Air Force, Navy.

Equivalent Military Job:

Air Force	Pavement Maintenance Specialist. (This is a broader job classification. As a pavement maintenance specialist you will be involved in maintaining airfields, roads, and drainage structures, and will be taught to understand soil construction and drainage problems.)
Army	Combat Engineer. (This is also a

broader job. As a combat engineer you will work on construction projects that give engineering support to combat units. This includes helping to build bridges and roads as well as working with minefields and demolitions.)

Coast Guard   Damage Controlman. (Another broad category. As a damage controlman you will be responsible for the preservation of modern safety and survival devices on Coast Guard vessels. Your duties may include welding, firefighting, pipefitting, and carpentry.)

Marine Corps   Combat Engineer. (Similar to the Army Combat Engineer described above.)

Navy   Builder. (As a builder you may develop skills in one of many trades, such as carpenter, roofer, mason, painter, bricklayer, heavy-equipment operator.)

Cook

General Civilian Job Information: As a cook you will primarily be responsible for the preparation and cooking of food for service to customers. Entry into the field is not difficult and usually involves on-the-job training or an apprenticeship, which may last about three years.

General Military Job Information: As a cook in the military you will be doing basically the same type of work as in a civilian restaurant, but it normally will involve preparing meals for a larger number of people, to be served in a shorter period of time. In addition, you may have to order supplies and keep records and accounts, and you may have to serve meals. Entry into this field is easy for those with the aptitude toward it. Basic cooking schools are available to qualified personnel prior to on-the-job training.

What are the basic qualifications for this job? You should have a strong interest in food preparation and above-average learning ability . . . be able to follow detailed recipes . . . have high standards of personal cleanliness.

Helpful High-School Courses or Experience: Food preparation, dietetics, business arithmetic, chemistry, home economics, hygiene. Any practical work experience in food preparation would be helpful.

Open to Women in: Air Force, Army, Coast Guard, Marine Corps, Navy.

Equivalent Military Job:

Air Force	Cook
Army	Food Service Specialist
Coast Guard	Subsistence Specialist
Marine Corps	Cook
Navy	Mess Management Specialist

Court Reporter

General Civilian Job Information: As a court reporter you will work in a courtroom taking down the testimony of witnesses and other information about trials or legal proceedings. Entry into this field normally requires special schooling, but is fairly easy once the schooling is obtained.

General Military Job Information: In the military your work in the courtroom will normally be similar to that of a civilian court reporter, but it may also be much broader in scope. Entry into this field is excellent for those with the basic qualifications. School training is normally provided.

What are the basic qualifications for this job? You must have a clear speaking voice to be able to use the stenomask, which is the usual method of taking down testimony . . . be above average in learning ability . . . have excellent eye-hand coordination, an aptitude for detailed work, the ability to work harmoniously with others, the ability to type or to learn to type.

Helpful High-School Courses or Experience: Typing, shorthand, bookkeeping, English, basic mathematics. Any work in an office, especially in a legal office, or as a typist or stenographer would be valuable.

Open to Women in: Air Force, Army, Coast Guard, Marine Corps, Navy.

Equivalent Military Job:

Air Force	Legal Services Specialist
Army	Legal Clerk. (This is a broader job classification. The legal clerk also may assist legal officers in the preparation and processing of court-martial records and help with claims studies and other special board proceedings.)
Coast Guard	Yeoman. (Another much broader job. The yeoman may perform a wide variety of administrative jobs, including the preparation and typing of letters and reports, the main-

Marine Corps
Navy

tenance of personnel records, and mail distribution.)
Legal Services Reporter
Legalman. (Still another broader job category. As a legalman you will be trained to assist professionals in the field of law. You will work in a legal office doing administrative and clerical tasks, which may include investigating claims, preparing subpoenas, and helping Naval personnel with minor legal problems.)

Cryptographic Technician

General Civilian Job Information: As a cryptographic technician you will generally work for a law-enforcement agency or a business that has the need to send and receive coded messages. You will use a Teletype or teleprinter equipment to transmit these messages and other equipment to code and decode messages. Entry into this field is difficult and usually requires special schooling.

General Military Job Information: In the military you will use highly specialized cryptographic equipment to code, transmit, and decode sensitive material. The specific duties are of a classified nature, and you will only be informed of them after you have qualified for training. School training is provided to all those qualified for entry into this field.

What are the basic qualifications for this job? You must be a United States citizen with a background that will permit you to get a high-level security clearance. You will need above-average intelligence . . . good eye-hand coordination . . . above-average speaking and writing ability . . . an adaptability to detailed work . . . a good memory . . . record-keeping ability . . . good vision and normal color vision.

Helpful High-School Courses or Experience: Typing, English, business-machine operation, electronics shop, physics. Any experience as an amateur radio operator, typist, telegrapher, or in electric or electronics repair would be helpful.

Open to Women in: Air Force, Army, Coast Guard, Marine Corps, Navy.

Equivalent Military Job:

Air Force	Radio Communications Analysis Specialist
Army	Cryptographic Center Specialist
Coast Guard	Radioman. (This is a broader job classification. As a radioman you will handle the transmitting and receiving of both coded and uncoded messages, which enable Coast Guard units to help distressed vessels as well as to perform its other functions. You may also maintain radio equipment.)
Marine Corps	Cryptanalyst
Navy	Cryptologic Technician

Dental Assistant

General Civilian Job Information: As a dental assistant you will prepare patients for treatment, care for instruments and arrange them on the tray for the dentist, and assist the dentist in dental procedures. You will keep dental records and perhaps work in the dental lab. You may also develop X rays, order supplies, and have general office duties. Special schooling is normally required for entry into this field. State certification may be required.

General Military Job Information: The duties of dental assistant in the military are basically the same as in a civilian dental office. Entry into this field is difficult except for highly qualified personnel. Basic schooling is available for those selected.

What are the basic qualifications for this job? You need an interest in dentistry and an aptitude for it . . . manual dexterity . . . emotional stability, dependability, and ability to work closely with others . . . a good memory and record-keeping ability . . . some physical strength . . . normal color perception.

Helpful High-School Courses or Experience: Biology, hygiene, physiology, chemistry, anatomy, and first aid. Any work in a dental office or a dental laboratory or a medical laboratory would be helpful.

Open to Women in: Air Force, Army, Coast Guard, Navy. (Note: The Navy provides all Marine Corps health services.)

Equivalent Military Job:

Air Force	Dental Specialist
Army	Dental Specialist
Coast Guard	Dental Technician
Navy	Dental Technician

Diesel Mechanic

General Civilian Job Information: As a diesel mechanic you will repair and maintain diesel engines used in trucks, buses, power boats, and the growing numbers of diesel-powered automobiles. Entry into this field is difficult and usually requires special training. As the number of diesel-powered automobiles increases, entry may become easier to keep up with the demand.

General Military Job Information: As a diesel mechanic in the military your work will be essentially the same as in a civilian shop, but the variety of engines you will work on may be greater. Entry into this field is not as difficult as in a civilian shop, and qualified personnel are sent to basic school courses before on-the-job training.

What are the basic qualifications for this job? You must have mechanical aptitude and the ability to read and follow technical manuals on diesel-engine repair . . . physical strength . . . good vision and hearing.

Helpful High-School Courses or Experience: Industrial arts, mechanical shop, auto mechanics, physics, English, mathematics. Any work experience in an auto- or farm-machinery shop or a bus- or truck-repair shop will be valuable.

Open to Women in: Air Force, Army, Coast Guard, Marine Corps, Navy.

Equivalent Military Job:

Air Force	General-Purpose-Vehicle Repairman. (This job is not restricted to diesel engines. As a general-purpose-vehicle repairman you will work on both diesel and internal-combustion-type engines and may also service front-end and steering systems.)
Army	Engineer Equipment Repairman.

	(This is also a broader job classification. As an engineer equipment repairman you may service the major parts of both wheeled and tracked vehicles of all types.)
Coast Guard	Machinery Technician. (A very broad job classification. As a machinery technician you may service both diesel and internal-combustion engines as well as work on propulsion boilers, steam turbines, and power-transmission equipment.)
Marine Corps	Engineer Equipment Mechanic. (Another broad job classification that includes servicing and repairing tractors, power shovels, road machinery, and other equipment.)
Navy	Engineman. (As an engineman you will operate, maintain, and repair both diesel and gasoline engines, as well as operate and maintain refrigeration and air-conditioning equipment on diesel-driven ships.)

Draftsman

General Civilian Job Information: As a draftsman you will prepare exact and detailed scale drawings from information provided by architects, designers, engineers, or scientists. These drawings normally include a number of different views of the object and information concerning the quality of materials to be used. Entry into this field is difficult and usually requires special training after high school and sometimes an apprenticeship.

General Military Job Information: As a draftsman in the military your job will be basically the same, but it is probable that you will work mostly in construction or mapmaking. Some of the services have basic school courses in this field, but most training is on the job, so those selected must already have preliminary training in the field.

What are the basic qualifications for this job? You must have some drawing skills . . . the ability to do detailed work . . . an above-average ability to visualize objects in two and three dimensions . . . excellent eye-hand coordination.

Helpful High-School Courses or Experience: Algebra, plane geometry, mechanical drawing. Any work experience in an architect or designer's office or a drafting job would be helpful.

Open to Women in: Air Force, Army, Coast Guard, Navy.

Equivalent Military Job:

Air Force	Site-Development Specialist. (This is a much broader job classification. As a site-development specialist you may perform construction-materials testing and plane surveying and also prepare engineering drawings.)
Army	General Draftsman
Coast Guard	Draftsman
Navy	Illustrator Draftsman

Electrician

General Civilian Job Information: As an electrician you will normally work with electrical circuits and wire installations to connect buildings with electrical power. You may work in finished buildings or in the construction of them. Entry into this trade is normally through an apprenticeship program which takes four to five years.

General Military Job Information: In the military, as an electrician you may do a number of jobs, including installing, inspecting, maintaining, and repairing low- or high-voltage electrical systems, power and lighting circuits, or other electrical systems. Entry into this trade is not as difficult as in civilian life, and those qualified normally are given a basic school course before on-the-job training.

What are the basic qualifications for this job? Mechanical aptitude with good eye-hand coordination . . . a good sense of balance for working in high places . . . the ability to learn to work with drawings and blueprints . . . normal color vision.

Helpful High-School Courses or Experience: Electronics/electricity shop, mathematics, blueprint reading, physics, mechanical drawing. Any work experience with electric wiring or electric motors will be valuable.

Open to Women in: Air Force, Army, Coast Guard, Marine Corps, Navy.

Equivalent Military Job:

Air Force	Electrician
Army	Electrician
Coast Guard	Electrician's Mate
Marine Corps	Electrician
Navy	Electrician's Mate

Electronics Repairman

General Civilian Job Information: As an electronics repairman you will repair all types of electronic equipment, such as computers, industrial-control systems, communications equipment, servosystems, and transmitters. You will test the equipment and apply your knowledge of electronics to diagnosing and repairing malfunctions. Entry into this field normally requires specific technical training past high school.

General Military Job Information: As an electronics repairman in the military your work will be similar to that in civilian life, but the variety and complexity of the equipment will probably be greater. There is a demand for personnel to learn this skill, and if you qualify, all the services provide basic school courses, plus on-the-job training.

What are the basic qualifications for this job? You must have above-average intelligence . . . mechanical aptitude with good eye-hand coordination . . . an aptitude for fine, detailed work . . . an above-average ability to solve mathematical problems and reasoning problems.

Helpful High-School Courses or Experience: Algebra, geometry, physics, electricity/electronics shop, mechanical drawing, English. Any work experience in radio repair, the mechanical or electrical trades would be valuable.

Open to Women in: Air Force, Army, Coast Guard, Marine Corps, Navy.

Equivalent Military Job:
Each of the services has a large number of highly specialized jobs that fall under the heading of electronics repairman. The job titles listed below are merely samples of these jobs.

Air Force	Integrated Avionics System Specialist
Army	Multichannel Communications Equipment Repairman
Coast Guard	Electronics Technician
Marine Corps	Microwave Equipment Repairman
Navy	Electronics Technician

Firefighter

General Civilian Job Information: As a firefighter you will assist in the fighting of fires. You will be trained in the use of firefighting and rescue equipment, rescue procedures, and safety measures. Entry into this field is normally through a mental and physical examination.

General Military Job Information: In the military your duties as a firefighter will be similar to those in a civilian fire department. There are specific minimum physical standards for this job. Some basic school courses are available to qualified personnel, but most training is on the job.

What are the basic qualifications for this job? You must have good manual dexterity . . . be able to work in high and dangerous places . . . have good hearing, good vision, and normal color vision . . . be self-reliant and able to work calmly under stress.

Helpful High-School Courses or Experience: General science, chemistry, mathematics, machine shop. Volunteer firefighting experience would be helpful.

Open to Women in: Air Force, Army, Marine Corps, Navy.

Equivalent Military Job:

| Air Force | Fire Protection Specialist |
| Army | Firefighter |

Coast Guard	Damage Controlman. (This is a much broader job classification. As a damage controlman you will be responsible for the preservation of modern safety and survival devices on all Coast Guard vessels. In addition to firefighting your duties may include welding, pipefitting, and carpentry.)
Marine Corps	Fireman
Navy	Hull-Maintenance Technician. (This is also a much broader job category. As a hull-maintenance technician you will do the metal-work and carpentry necessary to keep all types of shipboard structures and surfaces in good condition. In addition to firefighting your duties may include taking care of a ship's plumbing and ventilating system and damage control.)

Key-Punch Operator

General Civilian Job Information: As a key-punch operator you will use a machine resembling a typewriter to punch combinations of holes into cards, with each hole representing a code for words or numbers. These punch cards can only be read by machines and are used in computers and other business machines. Entry into this field is not difficult, especially if you have had any training in typing.

General Military Job Information: In the military your duties as a key-punch operator will be similar to those in a civilian job, but you will most likely have other duties in addition to keypunching. Entry into the specific job of key-punch operator is not difficult, but advancement into other jobs in the computer or data-processing fields is open only to highly qualified personnel. Basic school courses are available to those selected.

What are the basic qualifications for this job? You must have excellent eye-hand coordination and good vision . . . be able to do detailed and repetitive work with precision.

Helpful High-School Courses or Experience: Typing, business-machine operations, business arithmetic, business English, data processing. Any office-work experience involving typing or data processing would be helpful.

Open to Women in: Air Force, Army, Coast Guard, Marine Corps, Navy.

Equivalent Military Job:

Air Force	Computer Operator. (This is a much broader and more technical job classification. See the write-up on Computer Equipment Operator elsewhere in this chapter.)
Army	Card and Tape Writer
Coast Guard	Key-Punch Operator
Marine Corps	Card Punch Operator
Navy	Data Processing Technician. (This is also a much broader and more technical job, and it is also covered under the write-up on Computer Equipment Operator in this chapter.)

Light Truck Driver

General Civilian Job Information: As a light truck driver you will operate small trucks or cars usually doing local pickup and delivery. You may do maintenance on your vehicle. Entrance into this field is relatively easy if you can qualify for the necessary driver's license and have a good driving record.

General Military Job Information: In the military a light truck driver normally drives a vehicle of under three tons capacity. Your duties will be similar to those of a civilian driver, picking up passengers or making local deliveries. You will normally be responsible for performing preventive maintenance on your vehicle and possibly for minor repairs. Entry into this field is easy if you can pass the appropriate licensing test.

What are the basic qualifications for this job? You must have a valid state driver's license or proof of driving experience . . . good eye-hand-foot coordination . . . good vision and hearing.

Helpful High-School Courses and Experience: Driver's education, automobile shop, business mathematics. Experience in driving any type of truck or bus would be helpful.

Open to Women in: Air Force, Army, Coast Guard, Marine Corps, Navy.

Equivalent Military Job:

Air Force	Vehicle Operator/Dispatcher
Army	Motor Transport Operator
Coast Guard	Equipment Operator. (This is a much broader job category and as an equipment operator you may drive both light and heavy trucks

	as well as bulldozers and other construction equipment.)
Marine Corps	Light Vehicle Operator
Navy	Equipment Operator (This is the same as the Coast Guard Equipment Operator described above.)

Machinist

General Civilian Job Information: As a machinist your basic job is to turn a block of metal into an intricate part that meets precise specifications. You set up and operate most types of machine tools including lathes, grinders, shapers, and milling machines. Entry into this field is difficult and usually involves an apprenticeship of about four years.

General Military Job Information: In the military your duties as a machinist will be basically the same as in a civilian machine shop but with more emphasis on the making or repairing of parts. Entry into this field is restricted to highly qualified personnel. Basic school courses are available before on-the-job training.

What are the basic qualifications for this job? You must have excellent manual dexterity . . . the temperament to do highly accurate work that requires concentration. You must be able to reason well and solve problems . . . be average or above in mathematics . . . be able to learn to read technical drawings and blueprints.

Helpful High-School Courses or Experience: Machine shop, mathematics, English, physics, mechanical drawing, foundry. Work experience as a mechanic or machinist, or repairing auto and farm machinery would be helpful.

Open to Women in: Air Force, Army, Marine Corps, Navy.

Equivalent Military Job:

Air Force	Machinist
Army	Machinist
Coast Guard	Machinery Technician. (This is a broader job classification. As a machinery technician you may be asked to repair gasoline and diesel engines, refrigeration, air conditioning, and steam-propulsion equipment, among others.)
Marine Corps	Repair Shop Machinist
Navy	Machinery Repairman

Medical Attendant

General Civilian Job Information: As a medical attendant you will assist doctors and nurses in their duties. You may administer first aid, take care of patients, check temperatures and blood pressure, escort patients to treatment, serve meals, and perform other related duties. Entry into the basic jobs in this field is not difficult, but advancement requires specialized training.

General Military Job Information: In the military your duties as a medical attendant will normally require a higher degree of training than those in beginning jobs in this field in civilian life. You may be responsible for a larger variety of basic medical care, often without immediate medical professional supervision. Basic school courses are available for those qualified for this job.

What are the basic qualifications for the job? You must enjoy helping others and working with the sick or injured.

You must be stable and dependable under pressure . . . above average in learning ability . . . and able to learn and understand medical terminology and procedures.

Helpful High-School Courses or Experience: Biology, hygiene, anatomy, chemistry, psychology, first aid, typing. Any practical experience in first aid or work in a hospital would be helpful.

Open to Women in: Air Force, Army, Coast Guard, Navy.

Equivalent Military Job:

Air Force	Medical Service Specialist
Army	Medical Specialist
Coast Guard	Hospital Corpsman
Navy	Hospital Corpsman

Musician

General Civilian Job Information: As a musician you are basically a performer playing alone or as part of a group, band, or orchestra. The field is overcrowded and employment depends on talent and is often erratic.

General Military Job Information: As a musician you may perform in any one of the following: in a group, band, or orchestra, a marching band, or a drum-and-bugle corps. You may do administrative duties such as keeping a music library, or be responsible for rehearsal facilities. All the services have special musical groups that play specialized music such as jazz, rock, and classical, as well as military music. You must already have a high degree of proficiency with your musical instrument and take an audition before you can enlist for this job.

What are the basic qualifications for this job? You must be skillful on at least one musical instrument and also be able to play without sheet music . . . have the ability to memorize.

Helpful High-School Courses or Experience: All courses in music and music theory. Any experience as a school or professional musician would be valuable.

Open to Women in: Air Force, Army, Coast Guard, Marine Corps, Navy.

Equivalent Military Job:

Air Force	Instrumentalist
Army	Bandsman
Coast Guard	Musician
Marine Corps	Bandsman
Navy	Musician

Occupational Therapy Aid

General Civilian Job Information: As an occupational therapy aid you will assist the occupational therapist in programs to promote patient rehabilitation. You may instruct patients in such activities as woodworking, metalworking, ceramics, painting, and other therapeutic activities, as well as sports, exercises, and games. Entry into this field usually requires some specialized training past high school.

General Military Job Information: Your duties as an occupational therapy aid in the military will be basically the same as in a civilian hospital. There is a limited number of positions in this field and most training is on the job.

What are the basic qualifications for this job? You must be able to get along well with people and be concerned about their welfare . . . have a skill in an appropriate field such as arts and crafts . . . have good personal habits of cleanliness.

Helpful High-School Courses or Experience: Arts and crafts, teaching, biology, hygiene. Any work experience in patient rehabilitation, arts and crafts, or directing games would be helpful.

Open to Women in: Air Force, Army, Coast Guard, Navy.

Equivalent Military Job:

Air Force	Occupational Therapy Specialist
Army	Occupational Therapy Specialist
Coast Guard	Hospital Corpsman. (This is a much broader job classification in which your duties include assisting doctors and nurses in all aspects of health care.)
Navy	Physical and Occupational Therapy Technician.

Office-Machine Serviceman

General Civilian Job Information: As an office-machine serviceman you will repair and service machines such as typewriters, adding machines, and accounting machines. Entry into this field is not difficult for those with a talent for repairing machines. Most training is on the job.

General Military Job Information: Your duties as an office-machine serviceman in the military will be about the same as in the civilian job. Entry into this field is not difficult for highly qualified personnel. Basic school courses are available for those selected.

What are the basic qualifications for this job? You must

have mechanical skill and dexterity, including good eye-hand coordination . . . good vision . . . ability to reason out the solutions to problems.
Helpful High-School Courses or Experience: Shop courses, mathematics, English, physics. Any work experience repairing office machines, automobiles, or farm equipment would be helpful.
Open to Women in: Air Force, Army, Coast Guard, Marine Corps, Navy.
Equivalent Military Job:

Air Force	Office-Machine Repairman
Army	Office-Machine Repairman
Coast Guard	Yeoman. (This is a much broader job classification. As a yeoman you may perform a wide variety of administrative functions similar to those of a secretary or clerk-typist in private industry, as well as office-machine repairing.)
Marine Corps	Office Machine Repairman
Navy	Instrumentman (This is also a broader job category. An instrumentman maintains all types of mechanical instruments such as meters, clocks, and office machines.)

Personnel Clerk

General Civilian Job Information: As a personnel clerk you will perform office duties involving personnel records. Duties may include typing, filing, working with pay scales, recording absences, promotions, training status, and other personnel information. Entry into this field is not difficult and most training is on the job.

General Military Job Information: As a personnel clerk you will have about the same duties as in private industry except that you will use the particular system of the service you are in. Entry into this field is not difficult for those with an aptitude for clerical work. Basic school courses are available for those selected, but most training is on the job.

What are the basic qualifications for this job? You should be above average in the ability to read and understand the rules and procedures relating to various aspects of your work . . . be able to type accurately . . . be able to work with others . . . have the ability to do detailed and repetitive work accurately.

Helpful High-School Courses or Experience: Typing, business courses, English, basic mathematics. Any experience working in an office would be valuable.

Open to Women in: Air Force, Army, Coast Guard, Marine Corps, Navy.

Equivalent Military Job:

Air Force	Personnel Specialist
Army	Personnel-Records Specialist
Coast Guard	Yeoman. (This is a much broader job classification. As a yeoman you will perform a wide variety of administrative duties comparable to a secretary or clerk-typist in private industry.)
Marine Corps	Personnel Clerk
Navy	Personnelman

Plumber

General Civilian Job Information: As a plumber you will install, maintain, and repair systems for water, heating, and sewage disposal. You will connect fixtures and appliances for these units and service and repair them as necessary. Entry into this trade is normally by selection for apprenticeship training and is very difficult.

General Military Job Information: As a plumber in the military you will do the same type of work as a civilian plumber. Entry into this trade is not as difficult in the military as in civilian life, but the opportunities are still very limited, and only highly qualified personnel are selected.

What are the basic qualifications for this job? You must have manual dexterity and good eye-hand coordination, especially in the use of tools . . . be able to do repetitive tasks accurately . . . be able to learn to read technical instructions, drawings, or blueprints. You must have some physical strength . . . a good sense of balance and the ability to work in high or cramped places . . . be able to work under pressure.

Helpful High-School Courses or Experience: Mechanical shop, plumbing, carpentry, basic mathematics, physics, English. Practical work experience in plumbing, water supply, sanitation engineering, or a machine shop would be valuable.

Open to Women in: Air Force, Army, Marine Corps, Navy.

Equivalent Military Job:

Air Force	Plumbing Specialist
Army	Plumber
Coast Guard	Damage Controlman. (This is a

much broader job classification. As a damage controlman your duties may include welding, firefighting, and carpentry as well as plumbing.)

Marine Corps	Plumbing and Water Supply Man
Navy	Utilitiesman

Policeman

General Civilian Job Information: As a policeman you will perform foot or motorized patrol in an assigned area to protect life and property. You may also control traffic, give first aid, do basic investigative work, or be a jail attendant or guard. In almost every large city police jobs are obtained through mental and physical examinations and by placement on a civil-service list.

General Military Job Information: Your duties as a policeman in the military will be about the same as on a civilian police force. Entry into this field in the military is not difficult if you have the required physical qualifications and an aptitude for law-enforcement work. Basic school courses are available for those who qualify.

What are the basic qualifications for this job? All the services have certain height and weight requirements. You must be above average in intelligence . . . able to work under pressure and in dangerous situations.

Helpful High-School Courses or Experience: Courses in law enforcement, marksmanship, martial arts. Practical work experience in law enforcement would be valuable.

Open to Women in: Air Force, Army, Marine Corps.

Equivalent Military Job:

Air Force	Law-Enforcement Specialist

Army   Military Policeman
Marine Corps   Military Policeman

Postal Clerk

General Civilian Job Information: As a postal clerk you will work in a post office sorting and handling mail and providing customer services. You may be a mail carrier and deliver mail. Entry into the U.S. Postal Service requires a qualifying score on the civil-service examination. Some large companies have mail departments with full-time mail clerks.

General Military Job Information: Your work as a military postal clerk will be very much like that of civilians who work for the U.S. Postal Service. Qualified personnel must be United States citizens, and entry normally includes a basic school training course prior to on-the-job training.

What are the basic qualifications for the job? You must have a good memory and the ability to do detailed work and repetitive tasks . . . be able to keep accurate records . . . be good at arithmetic . . . be able to deal with people.

Helpful High-School Courses or Experience: General business courses, basic mathematics, English, typing. Almost any office experience or experience dealing with customers would be helpful.

Open to Women in: Air Force, Army, Coast Guard, Marine Corps, Navy.

Equivalent Military Job:
Air Force   Administration Specialist. (This is a broader job classification. As an administrative specialist you may

	be involved in a number of administrative duties other than postal services.)
Army	Postal Clerk
Coast Guard	Yeoman. (This is also a much broader job classification. As a yeoman you will perform a wide variety of administrative functions, including preparation and typing of letters and reports, maintenance of records, and court reporting, as well as handling personal mail.)
Marine Corps	Postal Clerk
Navy	Postal Clerk

Radio and TV Announcer

General Civilian Job Information: About 80 percent of all announcers work in radio. In radio you may do a variety of jobs depending on the size of the station. At a small radio station you may be required to have a first-class radio-telephone operator's license so you can double as an operator or technician. You may be assigned to work as a disc jockey, sportscaster, or newscaster. You may have to operate phonograph or tape play-back equipment, read from prepared scripts, present memorized material, or speak without prior preparation. There are no formal educational requirements for entering the field of radio and TV announcing, but jobs are hard to get, and you may have to serve as a studio employee while waiting for a position to open up on the broadcast staff.

General Military Job Information: Generally your duties as an announcer in the military will be the same as those at a civilian station. You may be involved in producing material for distribution to civilian stations or in the actual production of programs on the armed forces radio and television stations. Schools are available for the few highly qualified people selected for these positions, but most of them have had previous broadcast training or experience.

What are the basic qualifications for this job? You must have a clear speaking voice . . . be able to think clearly and speak your thoughts under stress . . . have an interest in current events and have a good vocabulary.

Helpful High-School Courses or Experience: Broadcasting, public speaking, drama, English composition, and typing. Any experience as an actor or an announcer would be very helpful.

Open to Women in: Air Force, Army, Coast Guard, Marine Corps, Navy.

Equivalent Military Job:

Air Force	Television and Radio Production Specialist
Army	Broadcast Specialist
Coast Guard	Photo-Journalist
Marine Corps	Radio and Television Information Man
Navy	Radio–TV Announcer

Radio Operator

General Civilian Job Information: As a radio operator you will work in a communications center transmitting and receiving messages using radio, telegraph, or Teletype equipment. Entry into this field usually requires special training in a technical school after high school.

General Military Job Information: As a radio operator in the military your job will be more varied. You may work in a communications center or in the field and with portable as well as fixed transmission equipment. Opportunities to enter this field are good, and basic school courses are normally available before on-the-job training.

What are the basic qualifications for this job? You should have above-average intelligence so you can learn the codes and technical procedures appropriate for radio broadcasting . . . be able to type . . . be able to solve problems quickly . . . have the ability to do repetitive and detailed work with accuracy . . . have a good speaking voice.

Helpful High-School Courses or Experience: Algebra, English, typing, electrical shop, physics. Any experience in amateur radio or with a radio or TV station would be helpful.

Open to Women in: Air Force, Army, Coast Guard, Marine Corps, Navy.

Equivalent Military Job:

Air Force	Radio Operator
Army	Radio Operator
Coast Guard	Radioman
Marine Corps	Radio-Telegraph Operator
Navy	Radioman

Stock-Control Clerk

General Civilian Job Information: As a stock-control clerk you will work in a supply room or warehouse making purchase orders, stocking supplies, and keeping records on stock received and shipped. You may keep records of financial transactions. Entry into this field is fairly easy for those qualified and training is mostly on the job.

General Military Job Information: As a stock-control clerk in the military your job would be almost the same as that of a civilian in a large corporation. Entry into this field is fairly easy for qualified personnel and usually includes a basic school course prior to on-the-job training.

What are the basic qualifications for this job? You should have a good knowledge of arithmetic . . . good handwriting. In some positions you must be able to lift and carry a heavy load.

Helpful High-School Courses or Experience: Bookkeeping, typing, business arithmetic, English. Any practical work experience in stock inventorying, record keeping, or the operation of office machines would be valuable.

Open to Women in: Air Force, Army, Coast Guard, Marine Corps, Navy.

Equivalent Military Job:

Air Force	Inventory-Management Specialist
Army	Stock-Control and Accounting Specialist
Coast Guard	Storekeeper
Marine Corps	Supply-Administration and Operations Man
Navy	Storekeeper

Telephone Repairman

General Civilian Job Information: As a telephone repairman you will make service calls and work as a lineman to install or repair telephones, wires, or cables. Entry into this field is not difficult if you are qualified, and most phone companies provide basic training courses before on-the-job training.

General Military Job Information: In the military your duties as a telephone repairman will be about the same as with a civilian phone company. Entry into this job classification is not difficult and normally includes a basic school course and on-the-job training.

What are the basic qualifications for this job? You should have good mechanical abilities . . . good eye-hand coordination . . . normal color vision . . . enjoy working with your hands . . . be able to work at heights.

Helpful High-School Courses or Experience: Mathematics, physics, electrical or electronics shop. Any electrical work experience is valuable.

Open to Women in: Air Force, Army, Coast Guard, Marine Corps, Navy.

Equivalent Military Job:

Air Force	Telephone Switching Equipment Repairman, Electro/Mechanical
Army	Manual Central-Office Repairman
Coast Guard	Telephone Technician
Marine Corps	Telephone Technician
Navy	Automatic Telephone Repairman

Weather Forecaster

General Civilian Job Information: As a weather forecaster you will study weather and atmospheric conditions and use special instruments to test humidity and barometric changes. The major employer in this field is the federal government, which normally requires technical training past high school before employment.

General Military Job Information: In the military you will perform the same duties as in a federal agency.

College-trained meteorologists are used for technical forecasting, but high-school graduates are eligible for entry positions and do low-level observations and forecasting. School courses are available for those selected.

What are the basic qualifications for this job? You should be good at arithmetic and be able to do detailed and repetitive work with accuracy, and able to learn to understand technical instructions. You should also have good eye-hand coordination . . . good vision with normal color vision.

Helpful High-School Courses or Experience: General science, physics, algebra, trigonometry, English, geography, typing, astronomy. Any work experience in the fields of meteorology, oceanography, or astronomy would be helpful.

Open to Women in: Air Force, Army, Coast Guard, Marine Corps, Navy.

Equivalent Military Job:

Air Force	Weather Observer
Army	Meteorological Observer
Coast Guard	Marine Science Technician. (This is a broader job classification in which you will collect and study oceanographic data as well as weather data.)
Marine Corps	Weather Observer
Navy	Aerographer's Mate

Welder

General Civilian Job Information: As a welder you may use both gas welding and brazing or arc welding to weld metal parts together according to work orders. Entry into this field is not difficult, but most companies prefer to hire persons who have had high-school or technical-school training in welding.

General Military Job Information: In the military the duties you will perform as a welder are the same as in a private firm, but usually the military job includes more than just welding. Entry into this field is not difficult, even though there are not many job openings.

What are the basic qualifications for this job? You must have mechanical skill . . . physical stamina . . . resourcefulness . . . good vision, including normal color vision.

Helpful High-School Courses or Experience: Machine shop, physics, mechanical drawing, welding. Any experience with welding equipment or metal cutting torches would be valuable.

Open to Women in: Air Force, Army, Marine Corps, Navy.

Equivalent Military Job:

Air Force	Metal Processing Specialist
Army	Welder
Coast Guard	Damage Controlman. (This is a much broader job classification. The damage controlman is responsible for the preservation of all modern safety and survival devices on Coast Guard vessels. Your duties may include firefighting, pipefitting, and carpentry as well as welding.)
Marine Corps	Metalworker. (In addition to welding you will also work with sheetmetal.)

Navy

Steelworker. (This is also a much broader job classification. As a steelworker your duties may include rigging and operating hoisting equipment to erect or dismantle steel bridges, piers, buildings, and the like, as well as welding, cutting, and bolting steel plates used in construction.)

CHAPTER SEVEN

How to Get What You Want When You Enlist

Want to know the best way to get what you want when you enlist?

Finish school!

And if you've dropped out already, get back in.

That's right. The services are more willing to invest the time and money to give you the training and the job you want if you can show them a diploma from a high school, technical school, vocational school, or anything higher. Why? Because numerous studies have shown that people with at least a high-school diploma have a better chance of success in the military than school dropouts.

It's still possible to enlist without a diploma, and although you might get what you want that way, the odds are against it, because you will have nothing to bargain with. And on top of everything else you'll find you have to score higher on the enlistment qualification exams than high-school graduates do. (This is the exam that finds out whether you are smart enough to make it, not the aptitude exams that determine your assignment.) It may sound silly to expect a nongrad to do better than someone with more education, but the way the services look at it, you may have had a good reason for dropping out—family financial problems, for example. Therefore, they want to give you the chance to show that you can learn the skills they want to teach you. The high school graduate has already shown the stick-to-it attitude essential to get through basic training and a technical school, but since the dropout doesn't have this track record, he has to show on the exam that he can keep up before he's given the chance to enlist.

If you dropped out of school you may have already discovered that you are not going to set the job world on fire. That paycheck that looked so great while you were in school now probably looks pretty small. You are probably in a job with no future, and will have to fight to keep even that. So the best way to get ahead is to go back to school—full or part time, day or night. Then, when you get that diploma you'll find you have something to bargain with to get the service training you want.

OTHER WAYS TO HELP YOURSELF

One of the best ways to prepare yourself is to join the Civil Air Patrol (CAP), or the Naval Sea Cadets, or the

Junior ROTC (JROTC) while still in high school. The services welcome men and women from these programs, because they have already proved themselves to be military-oriented, have basic military skills, and, since the programs are all voluntary, are obviously well motivated. Membership in any of them will give you outstanding promotion potential. In some cases they will earn you an automatic promotion to E-2 the day you enlist. That means you start off a rank ahead of the others in your basic class—and about $50 higher in pay. They also make you a more attractive candidate for specialized training and for faster promotions.

Civil Air Patrol

The Civil Air Patrol is a civilian organization sponsored by and partially supported by the Air Force. The CAP is involved in about 70 percent of the search-and-rescue missions in our country.

The Air Force assists the dues-contributing volunteers in CAP by providing active-duty liaison personnel to CAP units, plus aircraft, communications equipment, and other supplies that exceed the needs of the Department of Defense. Members wear a uniform similar to the Air Force uniform but with a special CAP insignia.

There are over 60,000 members in CAP, and close to half that number are cadets between the ages of 13 and 18. Twenty percent of them are female.

A major CAP program is flight training. There are also a number of courses conducted by the Air Force, the Federal Aviation Administration, and the National Aeronautics and Space Administration. The successful completion of a prescribed course of aviation study and attendance at one summer camp, held at an Air Force base, earns the cadet a Certificate of Proficiency.

If you enlist in the Air Force this certificate will earn you an immediate and automatic rank of E-2, and may give you the chance to bypass all or part of your basic training. The other services recognize this training, too, and may give you a promotion based on it, but a promotion is automatic only in the Air Force.

The Naval Sea Cadet Corps

This is a training program for boys and girls aged 14 through 17. It is sponsored by the Navy League, a civilian organization, and is supported by the Department of the Navy in much the same way the Air Force supports CAP.

A primary goal of the Sea Cadet program is to interest young people in serving in the sea services—Navy, Marines, and Coast Guard—and in this they have been very successful. Approximately 70 percent of the sea cadets enter the Armed Forces when they reach 18, and most do enter a sea service.

Junior Reserve Officer Training Corps (JROTC)

The Air Force, Army, and Navy all conduct JROTC courses in selected high schools all over the country. The Army, for example, teaches JROTC to almost 100,000 students in over 600 high schools.

Both young men and women can qualify as cadets if they are physically fit United States citizens at least 14 years old.

The JROTC courses are part of the school curriculum, and classes are conducted as part of your daily schedule just like any other class. The instruction is provided by retired officers and NCOs. All uniforms, textbooks, and equipment are provided by the sponsoring service at no cost to you.

Enrollment in JROTC does not obligate you to any future military service, but if you do decide to enlist, it will give you a rank as high as E-3 the day you enlist and may get you out of all or part of your basic training.

Another advantage is that competitive appointments to the Air Force Academy, Annapolis, and West Point are available to outstanding cadets. These are in addition to the regular congressional and presidential appointments.

JROTC prepares students to compete for college ROTC scholarships. And if you do go into a senior ROTC program in college, with or without a scholarship, you probably will be able to start in an advanced class.

A FREE TEST TO HELP YOU DECIDE

It's easy to see that different occupations require different abilities or aptitudes. And it is known that a well-constructed aptitude test can, with reasonable accuracy, predict the success or failure of an individual in a specific occupation. For this reason, all the services rely heavily on aptitude testing to determine your career field and even your specific job.

But you don't have to join up to find out where your aptitudes lie. Several times each school year the military offers aptitude testing to high-school students, free and with no obligation.

The two-and-a-half-hour test is called the Armed Services Vocational Aptitude Battery (ASVAB), and it is offered to you through the school officials and often on school time. It is called a *battery*, because it is really a combination of a number of specific aptitude tests. Your scores on different questions and in different sections of the test are clustered into composite scores that show your aptitudes in the following areas: verbal, analytic/quantitative, clerical, mechanical, trade/technical, and academic abilities.

The test's reliability in predicting a person's success or failure in a specific occupation has been high, and the reliability of the composite scores has proved to be even higher. Since the test is so reliable, it really can measure your potential.

The ASVAB is for high-school seniors, but lower classmen may, and should, take it. If you take it as a junior it means you get another crack at it as a senior, and just knowing how to take it may improve your scores.

It is not a pass-fail test. There is no passing score. Instead you'll receive a series of scores in the specific and composite areas that tell you where you stand in a rating of all the students who took that same test nationwide. What you'll get is a percentile score. If you score in the 65 percentile it means that on that particular test you scored higher than 64 students and lower than 35 students out of every hundred students who took the test.

Your scores will either open or close doors to specific military career training programs. For instance, if you apply for training as an air-traffic control radar repairman in the Air Force you'll need a score of 80 in the electronics part of the ASVAB to qualify. To apply for training as an Air Force machinist you need a score of 40 in the mechanical portion.

You should know that these qualifying or cut-off scores fluctuate with the supply and demand for each specialty, and that each service has its own cut-off score for each course. If you are just under the line in qualifying for the school of your choice in one service, and the differences in service life-styles don't make a difference to you, you might check the other services and find out if you are above the cut-off score for a similar school.

Even if you don't decide to enlist, the free ASVAB can help you to narrow down your career choices to a manageable number. By matching your composite and individual scores with your interests, you can make a more intelligent career decision.

The ASVAB results are normally returned to your school within 30 days after testing. Your school counselor will be able to give you a copy and interpret the scores for you. If you want additional information, take your test results to any military recruiter. There is no obligation in this, of course.

Although you can't study for an aptitude test, you will probably do better on the ASVAB if you understand the questions. To help you with this, the Department of Defense offers a free booklet called *ASVAB: Your Future Is Now.* You may be able to get a copy through your school counselor. If not, ask for one at any JROTC unit or recruiting office.

QUALIFICATIONS FOR ENLISTMENT

If you've gotten this far in this book, you probably feel that you'll be able to meet all the basic qualifications for enlistment. But just to make sure, here is the outline you'll have to fit into if you don't have prior military service:

Age. All services require you to be at least 17. Those under 18 must have a signed parental consent form to join. The maximum age varies from about 27 to 35, depending on the service.

Citizenship. You must be either (a) a United States citizen; or (b) a national of the United States, such as a native of American Samoa; or (c) a legal alien admitted to the United States for permanent residency.

Trainability. Most services require a high-school diploma or its equivalent. All of the services require that you meet certain minimum scores on the ASVAB or other entrance tests. The Coast Guard has no formal educational requirements, but evaluates your education and scores on your entrance tests.

Physical. All applicants must meet the current physical-fitness standards. These vary from service to service and for males and females, but if you are in normal health you should have no trouble getting in. Certain enlistment options, such as aviation, airborne, or submarine service, have more stringent physical requirements.

Moral Character. No one wants a "loser," so all applicants must be of good moral character. Moral failings that will cause rejection include: alcoholism, drug dependence, a history of antisocial behavior, a history of frequent or chronic venereal disease, and conviction for certain criminal offenses. Normally a simple background check is made of all applicants.

Dependents. You'll have little or no trouble if you have older parents who live with you, or if you are married, but if you are a single parent with a dependent under 18, you stand a chance of being rejected.

Note that there are a number of ifs, ands, or buts for each of these qualifications. Unless it is obvious that you are a "loser" and will be more of a problem than an asset to the service, the recruiters will try to get you a waiver that will excuse you from whatever requirements you are not able to meet fully. If you don't have luck with one service, try another. It's the law of supply and demand again.

ENLISTMENT OPTIONS: THE CHOICE IS YOURS

It wasn't too long ago that when you raised your right hand and were sworn into the service you were completely at the mercy of the people making assignments. Now it's a buyer's market, and you are the buyer.

If you know the ropes, which is what this book is all about, you no longer have to buy the recruiter's bill of goods on just his word. When you enlist you can get a signed contract in which the seller—the military service—guarantees to give you what you want. The key, of course, is that you must be qualified for what you ask for.

The services offer a wide variety of guaranteed options that give you a choice of training, job assignment, unit assignment, or duty location. Some of them even include substantial cash bonuses. There are also options that let you sign up now and go later, and a buddy plan that guarantees that you and your buddy will stay together at least through basic training and possibly longer.

You'll actually sign a contract for the options you want, and the contract is binding both on you and the service, so read it as carefully as you should any contract. After all, you are offering three or more years of your life in exchange for the guarantee, so it will be worth your while to make sure you understand exactly what you're getting yourself into.

Also make sure you understand what you have to do and with whom you should get in touch if you think the military is breaking the contract or not keeping it exactly as you understood it.

Samples of Enlistment Options

Here are summaries of the major options offered by the Navy and the Army in 1979. The Air Force, Marines, and Coast Guard all have options similar to these.

Options are designed to attract enlistees to fill the specific needs of the individual service, so they change as the needs change. As always, you should check with the recruiters for the current list when you are gathering information to make your career decisions. Even if these specific options aren't in effect then, this sample will give you an idea of the kind that is usually available.

Navy Enlistment Options

Delayed-Entry Option. With this option you join now and go later. Why would you want to do this? One reason might be that all the classes in the school you want are filled for the next few months. So you take a delayed entry, and then the Navy can guarantee you a space in a later class. You don't go on active duty until it is time for the boot camp immediately before your class starts.

A delayed entry can also be used if you are sure you want to join the Navy (or any other service, as they all have this option) but you want to finish high school or take a summer off before starting your new career, or if for any other reason you want to sign up now and go later. The delay can be up to 365 days.

A hidden benefit of a delayed entry is that the time between when you enlist and when you actually report for duty is counted toward your seniority for pay purposes. This won't make much difference until you are an E-3, but after that it'll pay off.

Nuclear-Power Field Option. A Navy career in nuclear-power propulsion is available to carefully selected high-school graduates. At present this option is restricted to men, but like everything else in the Navy, it will probably be opened up to women eventually.

After recruit training, qualified applicants attend a basic technical school in one of four specialties: electricity, electronics, interior communications, or machinist. Following this is a 24-week course in the Basic Nuclear School and then 26 weeks of nuclear-propulsion-plant training.

As a nuclear-power field candidate you'll be enlisted in the pay grade of E-3 if you sign up for six years, and will be automatically advanced to E-4 upon completion of the basic technical school.

Advanced Electronics Field Option. This is a specialized

six-year program open to men and women. If you qualify for this option you'll be enlisted as an E-3 and automatically advance to E-4 upon successful completion of the preliminary phase of the basic technical school in electronics.

Advanced Technical Field Option. This also involves an enlistment of six years starting in pay grade E-3. You are guaranteed assignments to both a basic technical school and advanced training. Seven skill areas are open: interior-communications electrician, hull-maintenance electrician, hospital corpsman, radioman, electrician's mate, engineman, and boiler technician. This option is open to women if the skill area is open to women.

Medical Technologist Option. Men or women with three or more years of college and courses in science and math can qualify for this option. This is another six-year enlistment starting at E-3. You'll attend Hospital Corpsman School, after which you will be promoted to E-4, and then go to an advanced medical technologist course, which makes you eligible for certification.

School Guarantee Option. This option provides a guaranteed assignment to a specific basic technical school. School assignment is determined by aptitude tests, personal desires, and classification interview before you enlist. You can enlist for four or five years, depending on the school you want to attend.

Occupational Specialty School Guarantee Option. Although the option just mentioned guarantees a specific school, this option only guarantees a technical school within an occupational area. The specific school is determined during recruit training. There are about thirteen occupational fields you can chose from.

Seaman/Airman Option. If you're interested in a firm assignment to sea duty or getting on-the-job training in aviation, engineering, or construction, this option offers those choices. Restricted openings for women.

Subfarer Option. This is a special program for men interested in submarine service. You must meet rigid physical and mental qualifications for this duty.

Direct Procurement Enlisted Option. If you have completed one or two years of vocational/technical training beyond high school that is comparable to the training in a Navy technical school, you may qualify for enlistment in pay grades E-2 or E-3. And if you have a minimum of two years' work experience in a trade that is equivalent to apprentice training or have reached journeyman status, you may be eligible to enlist in pay grades up to E-7. Specific eligibility requirements vary according to the occupational field in which you acquired your experience and school training.

Army Enlistment Options

Delayed Entry Option. This is basically the same as the Navy program.

Training of Choice Option. This guarantees your attendance at a specific formal course of instruction of your choice.

Airborne Option. If you're interested in jumping out of airplanes, this option is for you. It guarantees training in the basic parachute qualification course, provided you can meet the physical requirements.

Bands Enlistment Option. If you have musical talent and training, this option offers you the chance to be assigned to the Army band of your choice. This is not for the amateur musician. You will have to take a tough audition and get a recommendation by an Army bands' representative that you be accepted. Once accepted, you can expect to be promoted to E-5 within a few months after finishing the bandsman course at the Armed Forces School of Music.

Officer Candidate School Option. This applies to college grads only and is covered in the chapter on "How to Become an Officer."

Warrant Officer Flight Training Option. This is open to high school graduates and is also covered in the chapter on "How to Become an Officer."

Combat Arms/Area of Choice Option. If you like the outdoors and are interested in being in one of the combat arms—infantry, armor, artillery—this option gives you a choice of unit or overseas location. If you want to be sure to see Europe or some other part of the world, this is the option to look into. In 1979 the option was not open to women, but that might change.

Communications Command Option. This guarantees training in any one of a large number of specialties and assignment for at least 16 months to an Army-communications-command unit. Most of the specialties available under this option are in the communications and electronics fields, but major communications units are just like any other large unit and need everything from cooks and carpenters to helicopter repairmen, so this is really a wide-open option.

Cash Bonus Option. If you enlist for four years under the combat arms option and earn a specialty rating in infantry, armor, or artillery, you'll be eligible for a bonus of up to $3000. You can also earn a cash bonus if you enlist for training in a critical specialty. These specialties depend on shortages and change too frequently to list here.

The cash bonus is payable when you are awarded your military occupational specialty (MOS), which usually occurs at the end of advanced individual training (AIT).

Naturally there are some rules. The main one is that you must stay in that critical MOS for the full four years of your enlistment, unless the Department of the Army decides to move you out of it. If you ask to get out, or if you get in trouble, you'll have to pay back a proportionate share—whatever you didn't earn—of the bonus.

Special Unit Option. This guarantees training in any one of a large number of specialties and a firm assignment to a unit of your choice for a minimum of 16 months. You can get this with a three-year enlistment. The list of units includes most of the major combat, combat-support, and service units, including medical units and hospitals, all over the world.

3rd Infantry/Berlin Brigade Option. If you're interested in being the center of attention while serving in a combat unit, this is the option for you. The 3rd Infantry, called the Old Guard, is the Washington, D.C., unit, with duties that include participating in presidential honor guards and guarding the Tomb of the Unknown Soldier. The Berlin Brigade is our highly visible combat unit occupying West Berlin, Germany. In both units the qualifications for acceptance are high and, at present, are open only to men.

Station of Choice Option. The difference between the station of choice option and some others that sound like it is that this one guarantees training in any of a number of specialties and then assignment to any station in the *United States* for at least 12 months. You might consider all the stationing options, like this one, in conjunction with the Army's educational program, Project AHEAD, and pick a station near your choice of a civilian "home" college or university so you can start your program there.

HOW TO TALK TO A RECRUITER

One thing you must understand before you talk to a recruiter is that he or she is in the business of selling.

Recruiters are salesmen, and as with any salesmen they have the tendency to glorify their product, which in this case is their service. This tendency occasionally leads to extravagant—even untrue—claims and promises. If you take the recruiter's word literally, you may be in for a big disappointment and have a harder time adjusting to your new life.

Don't take that warning wrong. In truth, recruiters are carefully screened and are closely supervised, so you shouldn't think of them the same way you would a used-car salesman. It's just that they believe wholeheartedly in their product. It's their own life-style they are selling, and so they sometimes forget to balance out the good points with the bad.

You can learn a great deal from recruiters as long as you realize they have the tendency to oversell. It may seem that they are offering you a rose garden when what they are really offering you is a small plot of ground in which you can plant the seeds of your career.

To put their sales pitch in its proper light and on a practical level for your situation and circumstances, you shouldn't walk in cold to talk seriously with a recruiter. A casual, drop-in visit is fine, but when you start getting down to serious bargaining, you should make sure you are well prepared.

How to Prepare Yourself

You've already done a great deal of good preparation by reading this book. If you understand the information here, you'll be in better shape to deal squarely and intelligently with the recruiter.

Here are some hints on how to make the most of these meetings:

First, take the time to be sure. And don't worry about using up a lot of the recruiter's time. Recruiters are paid to give time to prospects.

Next, don't believe anything that isn't in writing. Even be a little skeptical of things written in brochures and other advertising. They aren't legal documents.

Realize that you won't get something for nothing. If you want training in a skill and a certain life-style, you have to be qualified for the training or have the potential to become qualified. So don't let the recruiter steer you toward a school you know is going to be over your head. If you do, you may flunk out, and that would void your contract and make you eligible for any assignment.

Realize that even if you have a guarantee for training or an assignment, your contract will probably include a time limit or some other type of limit. For example, a promise of assignment to a unit of your choice may only guarantee that assignment for a year or sixteen months, whereas your enlistment will be for three years or more. After that, you go where the military needs you, and you do what they want done.

Before you go to see the recruiter, write down the questions you want answered, and don't forget to take your list of questions with you. Use this book as a guide. If there's something in it that interests you, have the recruiter update it for you. You might want to take the book with you so you have it as a reference. (Some recruiters may tell you this book is no good, but don't believe them. It's hard to keep the details up-to-date, but the basic information and the concepts are from the recruiting commands, and the personal comments come from my own experience and that of other active and retired military personnel.)

Don't be timid in dealing with the recruiter, and don't let a recruiter intimidate or overwhelm you with his pitch. Ask questions. If you don't understand the answers, ask the recruiter to go back and start over. Don't be satisfied until you are sure you understand the answer. If it's an important point, it might be a good idea to repeat the answer to the recruiter in your own words to see if you really do understand it. If you are nervous or unsure of yourself, take along a parent, a friend, or a teacher. In fact, if you request it, the recruiter will come to see you at your home, at school, or just about anywhere you want, so you can make it convenient for someone else to be there. Remember, it's your career you're talking about, not the recruiter's, so it's essential that *you* understand, not that he or she understands.

Level with the recruiter. You expect him to tell the truth—*and most will*, despite my warnings about them— so it's only fair that you do the same. If you've had problems at school or with the police, if there is a medical problem or anything else the military might want to be aware of before enlisting you, let the recruiter know. And if a question on that subject comes up on a form you have to fill out, answer truthfully. A few recruiters, facing a quota, may try to persuade you to conceal facts, but don't let them. Unless it's something major like a felony, it probably won't disqualify you from enlisting, but if you conceal it and it comes out after you're in the service, it could cause you more trouble than it's worth. It might void your contract or even lead to a charge of a fraudulent enlistment.

As with any legal document, the enlistment contract is a complex and carefully worded piece of paper, which is drawn up to spell out both your responsibilities and those of the service. It is worded to protect you both from being cheated. But its commitments are binding, so don't sign it unless you understand every word in it.

Normally you won't sign your contract at the recruiting office. The signing will take place after you've completed your medical and mental exams at the Armed Forces Examining and Entrance Station. But the recruiter will be able to show you a copy of the contract you want, make preliminary checks to make sure you are eligible for it, and explain the terms to you. If you want, the recruiter will even give you a copy of the contract so you can take it to someone knowledgeable, perhaps even a lawyer, to have it explained.

One last thing. This whole section reads like a warning to be on your guard against the unscrupulous recruiter. And it's meant to sound that way, because it is your life you are planning. But—and it's a big BUT—the number of unscrupulous recruiters is very small. Most are hard-working, dedicated people who want to enlist only the best people into their service. The majority of them will be excellent career advisers and they can be real friends—as long as they know you know the score.

WHAT HAPPENS WHEN YOU ENLIST

At the Recruiting Station. If after all your investigating you decide to join up, you'll have to go to a recruiting station. Bring your birth certificate with you, or some other acceptable proof of when and where you were born. You'll also need your high-school diploma, or your school record if you didn't graduate, and your social security card. If you are missing any of these, call the recruiter, and he'll tell you what to do. He'll also tell you if you need any other documents, such as your wedding license.

At the recruiting station they will verify your age, citizenship, and social security number. That number, by the way, will be your military identification number too. They will then help you fill out a number of long forms that will ask you for information on just about everything that has ever happened in your life.

One form will be the "Statement of Personal History," which asks for such things as the names of all the schools you have attended, the addresses of all the places where you have lived and worked, the names and addresses of close relatives, the names and addresses of references who are not relatives, and a list of the sports you play. If you have a poor memory for details, you can pick up a copy of this form on an early visit to the recruiter, or call and they'll send you one, and you can fill it out at home, where you'll have time and where someone can help with the information needed.

Among the other forms you'll be completing are a "Statement of Law Violations and Previous Convictions" and statements on whether you are claiming any dependents for pay purposes, and even a statement that you understand all the other statements.

There will be a lot of paperwork, and the recruiters will give you a lot of information, but as already noted, you will not actually enlist at the recruiting station. The actual signing of your enlistment contract and the swearing-in ceremony will take place later, at the nearest Armed Forces Examining and Entrance Station, or AFEES. The AFEES is a joint operation where all candidates for enlistment in all the services go.

If you are going directly into the service, the recruiter will give you a one-way ticket on commercial transportation to the nearest AFEES. If you are going to be preprocessed for enlistment or will be reporting at a later date, you'll get a round-trip ticket. And if you have to stay overnight before reporting to the AFEES, you'll get vouchers to cover the cost of your room and meals.

At the AFEES. Up to now what you've been doing with the recruiters has really just been talk. The recruiter has done some preliminary screening to make sure you meet the general qualifications for enlistment, but it won't be until you finish at the AFEES that you'll know for sure if you are in or not. The AFEES is also where you'll get a firm word, and a contract, on the enlistment option you want.

First you'll go through a series of medical and mental evaluations and then you'll get into the final bargaining for your contract.

Upon arrival at the AFEES, you'll be greeted by an officer or NCO. Don't worry if he or she is not from the service in which you are enlisting. Remember, it's a joint operation. You'll be given a briefing explaining the various steps in your examinations and given instructions about meals and, if necessary, overnight accommodations. You'll probably spend at least one day and part of a second at the station.

Your processing will be divided into three general areas: medical, mental (if you haven't already completed all the tests at the recruiting station), and administrative. The examinations will be conducted by doctors and trained technicians, and the results will be evaluated by professionals. The military isn't going to buy a pig in a poke. It wants the full story on you before it signs the contract.

Your physical exam will include: height and weight measurement, vision testing including color vision, hearing tests, blood pressure, X rays, blood samples, urine testing, and an overall evaluation of your general physical condition.

Women are examined separately, and a female escort will be present.

If you're applying for something like submarine duty or airborne or aviation duties, you'll get a more thorough physical.

After you finish the physical exam you'll have a private conference with a doctor who will evaluate both the results of your testing and your past medical history. If you have any medical documents or letters that explain your condition, make sure you bring them with you to the AFEES and let the doctor review them. If any medical problems are discovered during the exam, the doctor will discuss them with you at your conference.

One hint: if you wear eyeglasses, be sure to bring them with you, and if you wear contact lenses do not wear them for at least 72 hours before the eye exam, because they can affect your score on the vision tests.

Assuming you make it through the physical with no trouble, the next step is the mental examination. Part of this is aptitude testing, and you should try to do your best on these exams, because they have a long-range impact on what jobs you'll be qualified for.

Next you'll meet the person and the machine who put it all together for you—the guidance counselor and his computer. This counselor takes the results of the physical and mental exams and your school and option request and puts them all into the computer. The computer will analyze all this, match it with the requirements of what you want and the needs of the service, and come out with either a confirmation that your option request is accepted or a suggestion for other training and options you may also be qualified for. If you are approved for a school it will put you down for a seat and let you know when the class starts.

The computer can do a lot, but if everything doesn't work out exactly as you want, the counselor is there to set up the closest thing to your heart's desire that the services can offer.

Then it's up to you. You can either go home and forget all about it, or you can agree with what the computer and the counselor offer you. In most cases, this will be exactly what the recruiter offered you.

If you do accept, then you're ready to sign the enlistment contract and finally raise your right hand and be sworn into the service of your choice.

The next step is basic training, at which we will take a close look in the next chapter.

CHAPTER EIGHT

It's Basic Training, Not Basic Torture

If you are a little scared about going through basic training (BT), welcome to the crowd.

You've probably heard a lot of old tales that are still making the rounds which are enough to scare anyone off. They are interesting "war stories," but most of them are no longer true.

Most veterans and older servicemen lament that BT today "isn't what it used to be," and they're right. There are several reasons for this. For one, BT in all the services now takes a shorter period of time than ever. Even the tough Marine boot camp was reduced from eleven to nine weeks in 1978. Another reason is that instructors are no longer chosen for their ability to kick sense into recruits.

In fact, it's against the law for any basic-training instructor to lay a hand on a recruit. Hitting a recruit is a court-martial offense, which means the instructor could go to jail for it. And, finally, perhaps the most important reasons are that enlistees in general are better educated now, and military teaching techniques are more sophisticated, so that it doesn't take as long to teach the simple subjects taught in BT as it once did. And the subjects are simple, because the purpose of BT, as the name states, is to be basic. The more complex training comes after you've passed this initiation.

WHY THIS CHAPTER?

This chapter has only one purpose: to give you enough information about each service's basic training to remove any fears you may have of it. Apprehension—worrying about what might happen—is often worse than reality. So if you can penetrate the unknown and learn about it, if you know what to expect, it can take the edge off your fears. That way you won't let your fears get in the way of your search for what each service can offer you in getting started on a career.

The important thing you should remember when going through this chapter is that you shouldn't let the ease or difficulty of getting through a particular service's BT influence your decision on which service you go into. The Marines and the Army have the toughest BT, but if either of them offers you the training and life-style you want, don't let their basic scare you off. It may be hard to believe when you're going through it, but the seven or nine weeks of discomfort will end, and will soon be just a vague memory—and probably not a bad one when you look back at it.

An Introduction to BT

The services agree that the main purpose of BT is to give you the chance to make a smooth transition from civilian to military life by teaching you the fundamentals of your new life. What that means is they will take your body and mind—both probably out of condition by their standards—and in six weeks or more reshape them into a well-conditioned unit filled with basic military knowledge.

Despite what you may have heard, the idea is not to turn you into a robot or break your independent spirit. The services want individuals who can think and act on their own in time of crisis, but the individual must first prove himself to be part of the team. As with any sport, you can be an individual star at the right moment, but you had better be a team player all the time.

The time each service allots to BT varies. The Air Force is the shortest with six weeks, the Army is seven, the Navy eight, and the Marines and Coast Guard nine weeks each.

The names they call basic training also vary. The Air Force calls it basic military training, the Army calls it basic combat training, and the Coast Guard, Marines, and Navy all call it boot training. The term "boot training" comes from the Navy and goes back many years. The traditional Navy bell-bottomed trousers—which, by the way, are returning at the request of the sailors themselves—were cumbersome during drill, so canvas leggings were put on over them, creating the appearance of high boots. And the term "boot camp" was added to the language of the sea services.

Depending on your service, you'll be trained with a group of fifty to one hundred men or women. This group is called a "company" in the Navy and Coast Guard, a "platoon" in the Army and Marines, and a "flight" in the Air Force.

In all cases you'll be placed in the charge of senior enlisted personnel, male or female NCOs, who will stay with your group and control every phase of your life, and almost every moment of it, for the entire BT period. These NCOs are also called by various titles, such as military training instructor (MTI) or drill instructor (DI), but no matter what title they go under, they have all been carefully screened and have gone through an extensive training program to make sure they know how to give you their best in training and counseling and how to get the best out of you.

There are certain things that are common to all the services' BT. For one, you'll get up with the chickens, or maybe before them, and put in a full day right up to "lights out" at night. You'll learn to be a meticulous housekeeper, with everything folded and stacked in a precise manner and everything spotlessly clean. In some services the males will go through the ritual scalping on the first day and periodically thereafter until graduation. (The Army officially stopped recruit scalping in late 1979.) And you'll learn the give-and-take required to live in an open-bay dormitory with up to fifty other individuals.

How Rough Will It Be?

How rough it will be for you depends on two things: the end product required by the service you chose, and your attitude toward the training.

As far as the end product is concerned, that depends on what your particular service wants you to know and feel by the time you finish BT. That is why Marine and Army training have to be tough. Even though both those services need technically trained people, they must still be sure that every trainee they turn out is physically, mentally, and emotionally able to stand up under the terrible strain of close combat and is able to kill an individual enemy, if necessary. They can't afford to coddle trainees. Coddling during BT could kill a trainee in combat. Their training isn't designed just to reshape you to look and act in a military way. They have to recast you in hardened steel. And even though combat-unit assignments are forbidden to women, at least at this writing, the concept carries over into their BT for women, and it is also tough.

Basic training in the other three services, although still rigorous and demanding, is not designed to turn out people who will meet an enemy face-to-face, so their training and discipline don't have to be as unflinching.

How to Prepare Yourself for BT

The majority of the recruits questioned near the end of their BT agreed that the trainee's own attitude had the greatest bearing on how rough it was.

If you go in with the idea that BT is both a learning experience and a test of your self-confidence—a test you're going to pass with flying colors—then you'll succeed. If you go in with a negative attitude, thinking this is all just a lot of junk that you don't want to put up with, then BT *will* live up to its old reputation of several weeks of hell.

None of the services wants to graduate a trainee with a bad attitude, no matter how smart that trainee is, because if the trainee carries that bad attitude over to his or her unit, he will undoubtedly wind up in trouble or perhaps even get someone killed. So if the instructors spot someone with a negative attitude, they have just two choices: work on the individual to change the attitude, or get rid of the trainee—either to a disciplinary unit or by discharge as unsuitable.

Good attitude is 90 percent of the ballgame. In many cases it can even overcome a slow mind or a weak back, because it gets the instructors on your side.

The other 10 percent of the ballgame, and something else you can work on in advance, is your physical condition. In this case, the graduating trainees recommend running as the best conditioning exercise to build your stamina before you report to BT. Running is a part of the physical training program in all the services.

If you've never run before, or haven't done it recently, you might start by jogging to get your muscles toned and to develop your wind. But as soon as you can, you should turn that jog into a real run. You're not out to make the four-minute mile, but it's better to push yourself before the training starts than to have the instructors push you during training.

If you have enough time before reporting to BT, try building up to running two or three miles. If you can get up to three miles in twenty-five minutes or so, you'll have the running in BT whipped. Not that you won't be urged to beat that time, but you'll have the jump on developing a better performance.

It will also help to work in advance on push-ups, pull-ups, and sit-ups. In the combat-training Army and Marine BT you'll do more of those than you can keep track of, but they're important even in the relatively easy Air Force conditioning program. And most instructors use push-ups for motivating you to do better in any task.

It's especially important for women to get themselves in condition before they arrive at basic. They will have enough to do adjusting to the hectic pace without being hampered by sore muscles and a dread of each physical-training period.

AIR FORCE BASIC TRAINING

For illustration, let's take a detailed look at what you can expect to have happen to you week by week in basic military training if you enlist in the Air Force.

Air Force basic isn't being used because it's typical—there are a number of similarities between the BT in all the services, but none can be called typical—but rather because the Air Force gets in all the fundamentals in the shortest period, just six weeks. You'll find all the elements of Air Force basic in the BT of each of the other services, just more of each element.

Every weekday about three hundred recruits arrive at the military training center at Lackland Air Force Base in San Antonio, Texas. Lackland is called the Gateway to the Air Force because all Air Force recruits receive basic there.

You'll be provided with transportation to San Antonio from the AFEES or your home, usually in the form of a ticket on a commercial airliner. At the airport you'll find signs directing you to an assembly point where you'll join the other recruits coming in at the same time, and all of you will board a bus that will take you crosstown to Lackland AFB.

You and the other new trainees will be called "rainbows" because of the variety of colors of your casual civilian clothes—a variety that will disappear as fast as a rainbow.

The bus will take you to the reception center, where you'll be assigned to your first military organization—a training "flight" of about fifty recruits. Air Force BT is the same for men and women, and many of your classes will be coed, but your flight will be either all men or all women.

Your new flight will be one of seventeen or eighteen in a training squadron—from 800 to 850 trainees. There are usually about eleven male and two female training squadrons in various phases of BT at any one time—over 10,000 recruits. The Air Force turns out between seventy and eighty thousand basic-trained airmen and airwomen a year.

Lackland AFB, your home for the six weeks of basic, is not a particularly large base in land area. In fact, it is dwarfed by Kelly Air Force Base, which it adjoins, but it has the largest population of any base in the Air Force. This is because of the large trainee population, both in BT and in technical and officer-training schools, and because the largest medical complex in the Air Force is on this base. With an average population of about 30,000, it would rank thirty-eighth among all Texas cities. It has four theaters, two gyms, three service clubs, twelve tennis courts, five chapels, a roller-skating rink, swimming pools, libraries, both a miniature and a full 18-hole golf course, and a museum. It also has about fifty aircraft, but no runway. These are old aircraft scattered about the base for display only.

But it will be several weeks before you'll be able to do more than just glance at most of these facilities and attractions as you march, or run, by.

You'll spend about half an hour at the reception center checking in, turning over the enlistment records you carried with you, and getting squared away in your flight. Then you'll get your first taste of marching in formation and your first taste of Air Force food as your flight is marched over to a mess hall to eat.

If you believed in the old-timers' stories about military chow, your first meal will probably be a lot better than you expected; however, you might be too excited to realize it.

If you feel a little scared at this point, don't think you are the only one. No matter how the others in your flight may look on the outside, you can be sure they are all as apprehensive as you are about the six weeks ahead. (Of course, after reading this book you'll know a lot more about what's coming up than those who didn't read it, and perhaps you won't be so apprehensive—and won't believe the stories of the know-it-alls about the square needles used to give shots.)

At the dining hall you'll meet one or both of the military training instructors (MTI) who will be your gods, guards, and guardians from now until graduation. The MTIs for a male flight will be either both male or one male and one female. For the female flights, it's reversed: either both female or a female and a male.

If you were expecting big, burly, tough-looking MTIs, you may be surprised. There are still some around, but many look more like a typical high-school teacher. Don't let looks deceive you, however; the MTIs know their job and yours, and they know how to keep you doing yours right.

MTIs are drawn from all Air Force career fields and serve in this assignment for a three-year tour. Many find the work so satisfying that they extend it, and some have made a career out of it.

The MTI will take over and march you to your dorm. At least one MTI will be on hand with your flight every minute for the first twenty-four hours, acquainting you with dormitory life and laying down the rules you'll live by during training. After those twenty-four hours you'll be under their ever-watchful eyes all during the training day and periodically on the weekends. And if one of them isn't around, someone else on the training staff will surely drop in to see that everything's going as it should. The faster your flight learns the ropes, the faster you'll be left alone during your "free" time.

One member of your flight, usually someone with prior military or military-school training, will be appointed dorm chief and will have limited but real authority in the dorm when the MTIs aren't there. It will be to your best interest to cooperate with him or her. The officers commanding each squadron are required to interview each dorm chief at least once every two weeks concerning gripes, harsh treatment of trainees, or other items of interest, so the dorm chief is your link to the commander.

For the next six weeks your MTIs will tell you when to

get up, when to go to bed, and just about everything you'll have to do in between.

Your home will be an open-bay dorm. "Open bay" means no dividers between the beds, and no privacy. You'll sleep on a cot about the size of a normal single bed, not a camping-type cot. And you will get to sleep. Air Force regulations say basic trainees are supposed to get a chance for at least seven and a half hours of sleep a night.

You'll learn how to make your bed in a military manner and how to keep your clothes and other personal belongings in a neat, military style in a locker. The MTI will start in right away showing you how fifty young people can live together without turning the dorm into a pigpen. The dorm will always be neat and clean because you'll keep it that way. The days when Mom was following you, picking up after you, are over.

Young men seem to adjust quickly to group living, but it is one of the hardest adjustments for women. It takes much more time for women to fit into a world with very limited privacy. However, most women agree that once the strangeness of living in a huge bedroom with two dozen or so other females passes, it becomes fun. The companionship makes up for the shortcomings.

By the way, this open-bay living happens only in basic. In regular units and most schools the dorms are divided into rooms, or at least cubicles.

The Training Schedule

Formal Air Force BT is scheduled for thirty training days. That's only Monday through Friday of each week, so to get in thirty days requires about six weeks. Informal training, conducted by the MTIs, will fill in some of your weekends.

Your first week of training will be hectic. Not so much because of what you'll be doing but more because of how you'll be doing it—in a military manner. You'll be stepping out of the civilian world you roamed around in so freely for eighteen years or so into a world of strict routines, punctuality, new sounds, new vocabulary, and a highly organized structure that crowds activity into every minute of your day.

When you look back at it, your first week will really seem like a breeze. Most of it will consist of processing and orientation.

The first training day you'll get paid. Not much, but enough to let you buy the standard items you'll need from the base exchange, with a little left over for pocket money. And if you're a man this is the day when you'll visit the barber for your scalping. (This may be changed by the time you read this.) You'll also be briefed on everything from what to expect in the next six weeks to the old reliable summer-camp standby, the buddy system. And you'll stop being a rainbow as you get your initial issue of work uniforms. You won't get your dress uniforms until later; first, because you won't need them for a while, and second, because they will be tailored to your shape, and your shape is going to change over the next few weeks. When the time comes to issue you the rest of your uniforms—which have a total value of about $300—you'll go through a series of fittings and fitting inspections to make sure that on graduation day the uniform fits you.

Medical and dental processing take place on the second

day, and you'll make your first of several visits to the dispensary for shots. You'll also start a series of aptitude tests and get your first formal class in drill.

Day three brings orientation, more testing, records processing, interviews to determine if you have any special or hidden talents, and another lesson in drill.

On the fourth day you'll get your second dose of shots, a class on Air Force careers, and an orientation of the physical conditioning program you'll start the next day. And on day five it starts, early in the morning, before breakfast. This is the first of thirty-two hours of physical training that slowly works you up to the point where you can run a mile and a half in about 14½ minutes if you are a man and 16½ minutes if you are a woman. This physical training program will be your wake-up drill about four mornings a week for the next five weeks. The fifth day will also include an orientation by the chaplain and one on dental hygiene, and, of course, drill.

Your first five days of formal training will be over, but your weekend belongs to the MTIs. They'll make certain you understand everything you learned during the first week from how to shine shoes and make a bed to how to plan your career and do sit-ups. And there will be at least one dorm inspection—more if your flight fails the first.

Your only excursion the first weekend will be to the chapel, if you want to go. Lackland, like most military bases, has services available for most religious faiths.

The second five training days include more testing and interviews, as well as drill and classroom work in subjects like military law—which you'll live under as long as you're in uniform—and Air Force customs and courtesies. From this week on, your days will be divided in half—classes in one half, physical conditioning and squadron duties (read that: work details) in the other.

The third week brings more of the same. The highlight, however, is payday. And if your flight is up to the mark, you may get base liberty, which means you can get out from under the MTIs for a while, but you will have to stay on the base.

The fourth training week includes your second issue of clothing, a multiple-choice test covering all classroom subjects to date, and the confidence course.

There are twenty different obstacles on the confidence course, which is about a mile long. You'll be required to make a score of 16 to pass. It's the same course for everyone, but women get a little edge on a couple of the obstacles that require arm and shoulder strength. Most of the obstacles require more coordination and stamina than pure strength. And, as the title denotes, they require self-confidence. It only takes a little strength to back over a small cliff and climb down a rope, but if you have a fear of heights you'll need a big dose of confidence to get over and down. On the average, fewer than one of a hundred men and two of a hundred women fail the confidence course.

Following this course, you'll take a total of ten hours of rifle marksmanship training and familiarization firing.

The fifth week your flight will join the other flights in the squadron to drill for the final week's parade and graduation review. Classes this week will include subjects like "Drug and Alcohol Abuse" and "Personal Affairs." The highlight comes on the weekend, when you receive a pass to spend the day in downtown San Antonio.

Then the final week is upon you, and with it come your

orders to your first assignment. If you are on a guaranteed enlistment contract for a particular school, your orders will come as no surprise; otherwise, you'll probably hold your breath until you find out where you are going. Over 90 percent of all basic trainees go to technical schools, either at Lackland or at some other base. The rest go to on-the-job training in a unit.

This week will be mostly taken up with your graduation parade, a final exam, and out-processing. Then you'll be on your way to your career training.

Does it sound like torture?

Statistically, over a long term, ninety-three out of every one hundred enlistees entering Air Force basic make it through. The other seven are discharged either because they have medical problems or they can't meet the training standards.

Once you become adjusted to the highly structured schedule, group living, and being subject to the mental pressure of military discipline, it really is just six short weeks of new experiences, making new friends, and only minor discomforts.

As one graduating trainee put it, "Keep your mouth shut except to say 'Yes, sir' or 'Yes, ma'am.' Keep your eyes open, be sharp and stand tall, and do what you're told when you're told, and you'll get through it with no problems."

BASIC IN THE OTHER SERVICES

Air Force basic training, I must admit, is not only the shortest in time; it is probably also the easiest. But a lot of what happens at Lackland also happens at the BT bases of the other four services. You'll get in-processing, aptitude testing, uniform fitting, drill, bed making and barracks cleaning, physical conditioning, tests, words of wisdom from the instructors, graduation parades, and out-processing. There are all these things and more, because the other services are not as technically oriented as the Air Force.

Let's take a brief look at what happens to you if you go through basic in one of the other services.

Army Basic Combat Training

Up until late 1978 the Army had separate training programs for male and female recruits. Now a change in policy puts them all through virtually the same basic combat training (BCT). Women are still not assigned to combat jobs, but they are trained to defend themselves with rifles, bayonets, and grenades just as every male soldier is, even if he is definitely heading for a rear-area job.

Army BCT is designed to turn out a disciplined, highly motivated recruit who is physically conditioned, qualified in a basic weapon, drilled in the fundamentals of being a soldier, and prepared for the next training step, which is advanced individual training (AIT) in either the combat arms or a technical skill. BCT is given at a number of Army posts scattered all over the country.

BCT lasts for seven challenging weeks. Or, as most recruits would say, "seven grueling weeks." Whether you're a man or a woman, you'll learn soldiering from the ground up. You'll learn to stand, walk, and march like a soldier. And you'll be trained to work and think clearly under stress and to make decisions under pressure.

The first few days in BCT are not too unlike the first few days in Air Force basic, except that you might find the drill sergeants a little closer to the way you imagined them— lean and mean. And even while your in-processing is going on you'll find you're already into the action. The Army realizes it takes time to build muscles and train minds to get the end product needed to accomplish its mission, so it doesn't waste a minute. You'll start off at a fast pace, and it will get faster. But it's a pace that millions of recruits have already proved can be handled if you put your mind to it.

By the end of the first week you'll be well into the physical-conditioning program; you will also have had a number of hours of drill and will already know a great deal about your all-important rifle.

As your body starts to firm up and your original self-doubts dissipate, the pace will quicken and you'll begin to feel a pride in doing the difficult tasks assigned to you. It will be a pride of achievement, a building of self-confidence that will make you ready for anything the drill sergeants can dish out.

For the first half of the program there'll be a steady diet of physical training (PT), bayonet training, and a whole week devoted to rifle marksmanship training, which leads up to your firing for "record" and earning a badge as marksman, sharpshooter, or expert. During this time you'll also learn the basics of how to live in the field. And one of the high—or low—points will be a PT test.

During the last half of BCT the tempo will pick up even more. But don't worry, if you've made it this far, you're already conditioned enough in body and attitude to make it all the way.

There will be night training, first-aid classes, guerrilla exercises, infiltration procedures, and all sorts of other training that you probably never realized existed. One thing you probably will know about in advance, because it is so famous—or infamous—is the infiltration course in which you make a long, low crawl under barbed wire and live machine-gun fire. Don't worry, the machine guns are blocked so they can't fire low enough to hit you, unless you're stupid enough to stick your head up for a look-see. You'll also learn land navigation, a high-sounding term for finding your way around in the middle of nowhere with a map and compass.

In the final week you'll take tests to see that you are up to the standards: combat-proficiency tests, physical-conditioning tests, and written tests on your basic military knowledge.

As with all BT programs, it all ends with a graduation parade and review, after which you'll probably find out that your drill sergeant is a human being after all, who even smiles.

Coast Guard Boot Training

The Coast Guard has two recruit training centers, one in Alameda, California; the other in Cape May, New Jersey.

Recruits are trained in companies of fifty-five to one hundred under the control of senior enlisted Coast Guard men and women. Men and women train together; only their housing facilities are separate.

Boot camp is approximately nine weeks of rigorous physical training (you need strength and stamina to work a small boat in rough seas), classroom work, and practical application of what you learned in the classroom.

Even though you may go to a technical school after boot camp, most recruits go straight to a unit first, so the Coast Guard wants to be sure they have prepared you for the potential hazards of its lifesaving operations. At boot camp, therefore, the emphasis is on teamwork, discipline, responsibility, and safety.

Since this is a sea service, boot camp also includes swimming instruction and tests as well as training in water-survival techniques that would help you remain afloat in the water for hours without tiring.

Because the Coast Guard is the smallest service, its basic training unit is also the smallest, so you can expect to get a lot of individual attention.

Marine Boot Training

The Marines are the Marines. There's no other way to say it. They have a reputation for being a proud and tough service, and they make sure that those who make it through boot training can live up to that reputation.

Recruits are under strict discipline in all the services, but normally, in basic, a recruit feels he's in a fundamentally friendly environment. It's sort of like going through an initiation period of hazing when you join certain high-school clubs. Not so in the Marines. From the minute you step off the bus at either the boot camp at Parris Island, South Carolina, or at San Diego, California, you'll be in an environment that appears to be deliberately hostile. The Marines do everything they can to make sure they separate the men from the boys, and the women from the girls, in boot training. It's a survival-of-the-fittest course that will push both your emotional ability to take it and every muscle in your body.

For women the program is not as rough as for the men, but the mental pressure to measure up to the high standards of the Corps is still there, and so it's not easy. Since most male Marines are considered combat riflemen first and anything else second, and since women cannot hold combat assignments, the basic training program for women is very close to that of Air Force Basic. At least that's the way it was in 1979. The Marines have already started to integrate basic officer training, so perhaps by the time you read this they will have also made boot training the same for both sexes. But until that happens there's not much need to describe women's boot camp. Just go back and read over the Air Force section and toss in a large dose of training in pride—both in yourself and in the Corps.

The training for men, however, is designed to produce that basic rifleman who is able to do his job on the battlefield and still display the highest standards of professionalism in garrison. Marine boot camp means physical conditioning, rifle marksmanship, drill, and discipline, and plenty of it, all aimed at building your self-confidence and pride in being a Marine.

Your drill instructor (DI) will be both like a parent and a devil in spit-shined shoes. He'll teach you to walk, talk, eat, wash, march, run, shoot; in short, he'll teach you everything except how to breathe. And he'll even teach you that when it comes to firing your rifle.

As in all the services, he can't lay a hand on you. But that isn't really necessary, because most DIs are past masters at giving tongue lashings that will make you feel you've been whipped by an expert.

As in the Army basic, you'll come under the gun right from the start. Even during in-processing you'll be learning how to be a Marine. Your normal day will begin before 5 A.M. and end whenever the law requires that you be given time to sleep. You'll learn a whole new set of skills: first aid, guard duty, how to drill with your rifle until it becomes an extension of your body, and marksmanship, the Marines' pride.

You'll also learn to overcome your fears. One place you'll do this is on the confidence course, a course that requires the agility of a monkey, the strength of a weight lifter, and the confidence of a Hollywood stunt man. For example, one obstacle is simply called "the slide for life." You start on a 40-foot-high tower from which four ropes descend at a 45-degree angle to the ground a hundred feet away. Your job is to crawl down these ropes to safety. Of course, if you are unlucky and let go, there is something below to break your fall—three feet of water.

Naturally, you'll spend a lot of time in the field taking combat training and amphibious and helicopter assault indoctrination.

And you'll be taught to kill. In fact, you'll practice it and perfect it as if it were an art—with your rifle hitting a 12-inch bull at 500 meters or your bayonet striking at a wooden silhouette, or with your hands. Killing is taught carefully and skillfully in the Marines, because this is the "first to land" outfit, and no matter what we all think of war, it's only practical and realistic to learn it as your trade and your salvation. Your potential enemy is learning it, too.

Then, after many weeks of down-in-the-dirt hard work,

you'll graduate, and you'll look back and laugh at your fears that you wouldn't be able to measure up to being a Marine.

Navy Boot Training

At any given time, about 7000 recruits are in training at the Navy boot camps in San Diego, California; Orlando, Florida; and the Great Lakes Naval Training Center near Chicago, Illinois.

The training is basically the same for men and women, and is broken down into three phases. Phase I is basic processing. This is much the same as in the other services, with the formation of companies of about 75 recruits, or "boots," clothing issue, medical checks, etc. A major difference here, as with the Coast Guard, is that Navy boots must take swimming lessons or pass a swimming test.

In Phase II you'll be given all the military training you need to understand what the Navy is all about and how to fit into it. This includes drill, physical training, classes in military conduct, first aid, safety at sea, and orientations on the Navy. There will be a number of sessions devoted to practical drills that are shipboard oriented.

At the end of this phase, those with orders to a technical school will go to that school. If you didn't choose to attend a school or weren't qualified for one, you'll go into Phase III, or apprenticeship training.

This is broken up into training for those designated to be either apprentice seamen, airmen, firemen, or constructionmen, and lasts from two to four weeks. Fireman apprentice training, for example, will provide you with a look at such aspects of shipboard engineering as the basic steam cycle and boilers and their operation, give you some basic information about electricity and generators and detailed information about damage control in the engineering area of a ship, and teach you the specific duties of a fireman aboard a ship.

The boots selected for constructionman training receive four weeks of apprenticeship training at Gulfport, Mississippi. This program differs from that given seamen, airmen, and firemen in that it provides a broad base in all the construction fields rather than the specific training of other apprenticeships. Afterward you'll report to a ship or unit for further on-the-job training and develop a specialty.

Some Final Hints About Basic Training

Even the easiest basic training may not be easy for you because of the psychological adjustments you must make to move from a civilian to a military life-style. But the more you know about it in advance, the easier it will be to make those adjustments.

Remember that in basic you are being trained to become part of a gigantic team. The slogans to remember as a recruit are "Cooperate and graduate" and "Don't fight the problem." If you cooperate with your group, it will be easier for all of you to make it through without difficulties and get on to the main business of starting your career training. And if you don't fight what you're told to do by the training instructors it will also be easier for you. This doesn't mean just not to buck them openly—you're sure to lose there—but also not to fight them mentally, because the anguish isn't worth it. As mentioned before, you can be an individual after you're finished your training.

Most important of all, pick your service by the choices it offers you in career training and life-style. Don't reject it because you're afraid of its basic training, and don't pick it because it has a "ladies and gentlemen's" basic. Sometimes the hard way is the best way and the easy way is the wrong way. It all depends on you. Nothing good comes easy. You can do it, and when you do, you'll be a better person for it.

CHAPTER NINE

How to Become an Officer

There are many paths you can follow in our armed forces to prepare yourself for a civilian career. Among those you should consider are the paths that lead to becoming an officer.

Surveys have shown that although officers often put in longer hours and work harder than their civilian counterparts, they are happy in their work. Job satisfaction is very high. Perhaps one of the reasons for this is that an officer starts out as a boss. Officers start at what would be considered middle management in the business world.

Another point is that in civilian life it is not unusual for a person to be stuck at the same level of responsibility for ten or fifteen years and become bored and frustrated. This rarely happens in the military. With promotions and reassignments come more responsibility and authority as well as more opportunities to make full use of your potential.

Even if you look at your military time only as a training ground for a civilian career, being an officer for that time has certain advantages over being in the enlisted ranks. For one thing, a new second lieutenant or ensign (0-1) starts out at just a little shy of $13,000 a year in pay and allowances. An enlisted man would have to be an E-6 with over eight years' service to make a comparable amount.

And looking past your service days to when you're job hunting, a successful three-or-more-years' tour of active duty as an officer is more impressive than the same time as an enlisted man. Private industry realizes that during that time you've not only received school training but have also had the opportunity to learn and practice the principles of leadership and management under all kinds of circumstances.

It's not easy to become an officer. In fact, with just one current exception, all the paths for someone just entering the service lead through college. You have to go on with your education and earn a degree. The one exception, which will be covered below, is the Army's Warrant Officer Flight Training Program.

But don't be discouraged by this college requirement. The military offers many different programs to help you get a college degree if you really want one.

Before we get into those programs, however, let's take a look at the two classifications of officers.

The Two Officer Classifications

Officers are divided into two distinct categories: commissioned and warrant.

Commissioned officers are those starting with the rank of second lieutenant or ensign (0-1). They have a "commission" from the President to be an officer. Commissioned officers may be specialists in a certain career field, but they are also trained in general managerial skills, so they can work their way up to serve in high-level managerial positions that involve the supervision and leadership of many specialties.

It is possible to become a commissioned officer without a college degree, but only under exceptional circumstances and after years of service.

On the other hand, a degree is not usually required to become a warrant officer. Experience is what counts. Most of the services have requirements for supervisory personnel who possess high technical skills and are able to assume positions of great responsibility that do not lead to high-level management jobs. These positions are filled by personnel who get their authority and rank from a "warrant" and so are called warrant officers.

Warrant officers are in a separate rank category that is above the highest enlisted grade (E-9) but below the lowest commissioned officer grade (0-1). They are addressed as "Mister," and are entitled to the salute and all the other courtesies extended to a commissioned officer.

Normally warrant officers are promoted up through the ranks, which is how they get their experience. The one exception, and the only one open to first-term enlistees, is the Army's Warrant Officer Flight Training Program, which you can enter from high school.

The One Exception

The Army favors applicants with at least two years of college for the Warrant Officer Flight Training Program, but your high-school diploma will open the door. Not that acceptance is easy for anyone: You must be between the ages of 18 and 28 at the time of application, attain a very high score on the Army Classification Battery aptitude tests, and pass both the Warrant Officer Aptitude Selection Test and a Class I flight physical.

If you make it through all that and are accepted into the program, you will still have to go through basic training with all the other recruits, but then you'll go on to a 42-week course designed to turn you into an Army aviator—probably a helicopter pilot. At graduation you'll get both the Army flight wings and the rank of W-1 with a pay base of over $700 a month plus allowances and flight pay, which will bring your total to well over $1000 a month.

So much for warrant officers. The rest of this chapter deals only with programs leading to commissions.

WAYS TO BECOME AN OFFICER

How would you like to get a free college education worth up to $100,000, get paid almost $5000 a year while you're going to college, and have a sure and steady job waiting for you after graduation?

More than 15,000 students are doing that right now at the four United States military academies.

Several thousand more students are getting tuition, books, and fees paid by Uncle Sam while earning a thousand tax-free dollars a year studying for degrees in civilian colleges and universities on Reserve Officer Training Corps (ROTC) scholarships. And others are getting some financial assistance by participating in the ROTC in a non-scholarship status.

The military academies and the ROTC programs are just two of the paths you can follow to become an officer. In addition there are special programs such as the Navy's Nuclear Propulsion Officer Candidates Program and the Marines' Platoon Leaders' Class, and the Officer Candidate Schools of each of the five services.

The Academies

You can get the most financial help—in fact, everything is paid for—if you are selected for an appointment to one of the service academies.

These schools for the professional are: the United States Military Academy, also called by its location, West Point; the Air Force Academy; the Coast Guard Academy; and the Naval Academy, which is also called by its location, Annapolis. There is a fifth, the Merchant Marine Academy, but since it is a civilian school that does not guarantee a commission to graduates, it will be discussed only briefly, just enough so you have a complete picture of all the opportunities available to you.

The Marines do not have a separate academy but get a share of Naval Academy graduates.

The Coast Guard Academy is controlled by the Department of Transportation and the Merchant Marine Academy by the Department of Commerce. The other three are all under the Department of Defense.

Right from the start you should understand that although your education at an academy may be free, it does not come cheap in relation to your time, effort, and personal freedom. You'll work hard to get your degree, probably harder than you'd work in a civilian university. Unlike the relatively carefree and independent life-style of the average student at a civilian school, every aspect of your life as a cadet or midshipman will be detailed out for you. You'll be up at dawn and deeply involved in studies, athletics, extracurricular activities, and military activities until late in the evening. Even your free time will be fenced in by limits on where you can go and what you can do.

It's a tough program, and generally one out of three entering doesn't make it. Some flunk out because of the demanding academic schedule, but most quit on their own because they can't adjust to the regulated life.

If you do like it, and obviously two out of three do, and you last out, you'll get a Bachelor of Science degree and an education that will stand up well in any career, in or out of uniform.

As far as pay goes, while you're in an academy you'll get an allowance (which means it's tax-free) equal to half the base pay of an 0-1. That amounts to about $5000 a year at current pay scales, or over $20,000 for the four years. Of course, that's not all gravy. You have obligations such as paying for your own uniforms, books, and supplies. In most academies you'll be put on a budget to cover these necessities and still give you some pocket money. And in some cases this budget will include mandatory savings to make sure you have at least $1000 when you graduate and have to go out and face the real world of your first assignment. (Under the budget system at the Coast Guard Academy, this graduation bundle is often several thousand dollars.)

And, as mentioned, there's that steady job waiting. In fact, your free education will obligate you to a contract to serve a minimum of six years. At present that six years means five years of active duty and one year in the Reserves, but the requirement fluctuates.

Don't look at that contract obligation as punishment or paying off a debt. You'll have a good job with good pay and many chances for advancement and for more education. And, as said, if you decide to leave the service after your contract period, you'll be welcome in the labor market.

Just in case you hesitate to go the academy route because you don't think they measure up academically, it's interesting to note that the U.S. Military Academy ranks near the top in the nation in the number of Rhodes Scholars it has produced.

The Air Force Academy

The Air Force Academy is located near Colorado Springs, Colorado, on about 18,000 acres of former ranch land. Dominating the western side of the reservation are majestic Rocky Mountains, with the well-known Pike's Peak in the distance. The sweeping plains are to the east.

Each year this academy accepts about 1500 young people interested in Air Force careers. About 10 percent of them are women. (You could attend this academy even if you want a career in another service. A number of graduates of the Air Force, Army, and Navy academies may choose to be commissioned in another service. For example, an Air Force Academy graduate could ask for an Army commission, and vice versa. There are restrictions, but it is possible to do this.)

Here you'll earn your degree in one of four academic areas: basic science, engineering science, the humanities, or social sciences.

The majors offered are: aeronautical engineering, astronautical engineering, basic sciences, behavioral sciences, chemistry, civil engineering, electrical engineering, engineering mechanics, engineering sciences, general engineering, life sciences, mathematics, physics, economics, general studies, geography, history, humanities, international affairs, and management.

The training for new cadets starts the summer before the first fall term, with a strenuous program of conditioning and field training. This is designed to build your strength and stamina as well as orient you to both military and academy life. Upperclassmen conduct the summer session.

During the academic year you'll attend four fifty-minute classes or study periods each morning, and three more after the noon meal. Unless you participate in intercollegiate athletics, and there are eighteen sports available in this, you will play on an intramural team two afternoons a week after classes. The other three afternoons are spent in drill, extracurricular activities, or study. There are more than seventy-five extracurricular activities available, ranging from work at the cadet radio station to the Rodeo Club.

If you feel you need academic help you may volunteer for additional instruction, which is conducted immediately after the class day.

After dinner you are required to study either in your room or in the library. You must be in bed at "taps" unless you have special permission to study late.

A typical daily schedule for Monday through Friday might read something like this:

6:35 A.M. (0635 military time) Reveille
7:00–7:20 (0700–0720) Breakfast
7:30–11:20 (0730–1120) Classes or study periods
11:40 (1140) Lunch Assembly/Parade
11:55–12:20 (1155–1220) Lunch
12:40–3:30 (1240–1530) Classes or study periods
4:00–5:30 (1600–1730) Sports/ Extracurricular Activities/ Drill/ Study
6:35–7:00 (1835–1900) Dinner
7:15–8:00 (1915–2000) Military/Activities
8:00–11:00 (2000–2300) Study
11:00 P.M. (2300) Taps

Saturday mornings are devoted to parades, inspections, training, or study. Saturday afternoons and Sundays are usually free.

Although cadets and midshipmen are usually restricted in where they can go during their free time at all the academies, none of them are cloistered. There are plenty of coeds around on the weekends, with dates brought in from surrounding schools and towns.

You'll have training again the summer after your freshman year, as you will every summer. This first summer you'll take SERE training. That stands for survival, evasion, resistance, and escape. That summer you will also take part in a special three-week program of your choice, which could be anything from sailplane soaring to parachute training.

The next two summers you may find yourself assigned to an Air Force unit for several weeks of indoctrination or receiving an introduction to flying in jet trainers, or taking part in any number of other activities. Those who volunteer for flight training after graduation spend part of each summer taking a flying program.

And, of course, you will normally get about three weeks' leave each summer.

The Military Academy

The United States Military Academy (USMA) is where the Army trains its professional officers. The campus is at West Point, New York, some fifty miles north of New York City. It is framed by the Hudson highlands and overlooks the Hudson River. The school itself is on about 2,500 acres, but it is part of a larger reservation of almost 16,000 acres.

The academic curriculum at the USMA, like that of the other academies, consists of two parts: a prescribed core program and an individually tailored program of electives. The core program contains courses necessary to give you a broad general education, whereas the electives let you study in areas of your own special interests or aptitudes. If you wish, you may elect to concentrate your studies in one of four broad areas: applied science and engineering, basic sciences, the humanities, or national security and public affairs.

As with the other academies, the overall program is a unique blend of demanding academic studies and military/adventure training, supplemented by a vigorous athletic and physical-education program and over seventy organized extracurricular activities.

Most military and adventure training takes place during the summers. The setup is similar to the Air Force Academy, with new cadet barracks run by upperclassmen during the summer before the first academic, or "plebe," year and then a variety of things to do each of the other summers. Adventure training includes mountaineering and survival training, flight school, airborne school, northern warfare school in Alaska, jungle-warfare school, and Ranger training. One summer you will also be assigned a junior officer leadership position in an active Army unit in the United States or overseas. The final summer you'll spend a couple of weeks on a senior trip visiting major Army installations in the United States and Europe and then return to start the cycle over for the new plebes in the new cadet barracks.

The typical day and various activities described in the Air Force Academy section are similar to what you can expect at West Point and the other academies.

The Coast Guard Academy

Only about 350 young men and women enter this, the smallest of the academies, each year. The campus is at New London, Connecticut. It sits by a quiet river among woods and soft rolling hills, and it looks like most other small college campuses.

The Academy offers majors in marine engineering, ocean engineering, electrical engineering, civil engineering, marine science, mathematical sciences, physical sciences, management, and government.

Summers are devoted to professional training, either afloat or ashore. If it is afloat, it might be on a cutter or on *The Eagle*, one of the few tall sailing ships remaining in the world. This three-masted sailing classroom is 295 feet long, with fore and aft masts measuring 143 feet from the deck. It can use 21,000 square feet of sail, supported by 150 miles of standard rigging. The ship's maximum sailing speed is 18 knots. It's a real sailing experience to travel on this bark, but you won't have to rough it like the old-time sailors. The crew's quarters are air-conditioned, the sails are made of Dacron, the windlasses used for hoisting sails are electric, and there are also a dishwasher, two radars, and a sophisticated communications room aboard.

You will take several cruises on this ship.

Summer training will also include work on seamanship, navigation, firefighting, aircraft operations, and duty with Coast Guard units in your special field of interest.

The Naval Academy

The Naval Academy is the only one with a definite mission to turn out officers for two services—the Navy and the Marines.

This school is located on the Severn River at Annapolis, Maryland, near Chesapeake Bay.

In keeping with the Navy's technological orientation, the emphasis at Annapolis is on technical fields of study. About 40 percent of the midshipmen major in one of the engineering areas: aerospace, electrical, general, marine, mechanical, ocean, and systems engineering. About 30 percent major in one of the physical sciences, mathematics, or operations research, 20 percent in the social sciences or humanities, and the final 10 percent in management.

As with the Coast Guard, summer training is both ashore and afloat and includes training and indoctrination aboard all types of naval ships, but mainly combat ships, and at various naval installations around the world.

The Merchant Marine Academy

The Merchant Marine Academy, located at Kings Point, New York, trains officers for our commercial fleets. Graduates receive either a third mate's or a third assistant engineer's license. If you take the required naval science courses you may apply for a commission as an ensign in the Naval Reserve or the Coast Guard.

The academy at Kings Point is a federal school, but there are five state maritime academies that offer the same opportunities for a Navy or Coast Guard commission. They are the state academies at: Vallejo, California; Castine, Maine; Buzzards Bay, Massachusetts; Fort Schuyler, New York; and Galveston, Texas.

How to Get an Academy Appointment

The Coast Guard Academy is the only one that offers appointments based solely on an annual nationwide competition. All the others require an official nomination by a member of Congress or another designated official or under a special quota.

Anyone who feels qualified for the Coast Guard Academy may enter the competition. Selection is based on your scores on either the College Board Scholastic Aptitude Test (SAT) or the American College Testing

Assessment (ACT), plus your high-school academic record and your record of participation and leadership in extracurricular activities. You must also have three years of math and three of English. To be competitive you should rank in the top quarter of your class, but if you are not in the top quarter but have shown leadership potential, you still have a chance, because the Coast Guard, like all the services, is looking for well-rounded young men and women, not just scholars.

The Air Force, Army, and Navy academies all require an official nomination before you can be considered for an appointment. A majority of these nominations come from members of Congress; each senator and representative may nominate an allotted number of candidates.

If you are interested in attending one of these academies, you should start the application process about a year before graduation. You don't have to know your congressman to ask for a nomination. Simply write him or her a letter, *similar* to the following. (You don't have to follow exactly, just follow the general format.)

Honorable (*Senator's Name*)
United States Senate
Washington, D.C. 20510

Dear Senator (*Name*):

or if you're requesting a nomination from the Representative of your Congressional district:

Honorable (*Representative's Name*)
House of Representatives
Washington, D.C. 20515

Dear (Mr./Mrs./Ms.) (Name):

It is my desire to attend the —— Academy and to serve as an officer in the United States ——. I respectfully request that I be considered as one of your nominees for the next class that enters the Academy.

The following personal data is furnished for your information:

Name: (Your official name as recorded on your birth certificate.)

Address: (Street, City, County, State, Zip Code.)

Phone: (Area code and number.)

Date of Birth: (From birth certificate.)

Parents' Names: (Father's name and mother's maiden name.)

High School(s) Attended: (List all if more than one.)

Date of High School Graduation: (If you're still in school give month and year you'll graduate.)

Approximate Grade Average: (If you don't know, get it from your school.)

Social Security Number: (If you don't have one, get one.)

I have been active in the high-school extracurricular activities shown on the attached list. (Attach list and indicate briefly your accomplishments and any leadership positions you held.)

My reasons for wanting to enter the Academy are: (Briefly and honestly state your reasons.)

I will greatly appreciate your consideration of this request for your nomination.

Sincerely,

(Signature)
(Typed or printed name)

Expect a Competitive Exam

Usually there are so many applicants that the members of Congress may require you to take a competitive exam with the other applicants to help determine who will get the nominations.

If you don't make a congressional nomination, there are other paths to try. Academy nominations are also available from the President, Vice President, honor military and naval schools, and the District of Columbia and territories (if you live there), and through the Junior Reserve Officers' Training Corps, among others.

Once you receive the nomination, you'll have to pass a stiff medical exam and a physical aptitude test, and achieve certain minimum scores on either the SAT or ACT before you receive the final appointment.

All nominations for the Merchant Marine Academy are made by members of Congress. The same kind of letter can be used.

Competition for all academy appointments is keen, but if you are in the upper 40 percent of your class and enjoy and participate in sports and other extracurricular activities, or held a part-time job while in school, you stand a good chance of being selected.

Where to Get More Information

If you are interested in trying to get into any one of the five academies, you should write them for information as early as possible in your junior year. These are the addresses:

Registrar, U.S. Air Force Academy, Colorado 80840.

Director of Candidate Guidance, U.S. Naval Academy, Annapolis, Maryland 21402.

Admissions, U.S. Military Academy, West Point, New York 10996.

Admissions, U.S. Coast Guard Academy, New London, Connecticut 06320.

Admissions, U.S. Merchant Marine Academy, Kings Point, New York 11024.

Academy Prep Schools

If you are nominated but fail to receive an appointment to one of the Department of Defense academies, there is still hope. You may be able to attend one of the academy preparatory schools and take another crack at it the following year.

The Air Force, Army, and Navy all run these schools to help prepare likely candidates to make their academy. There is a catch, however; these academies are run for people who are already in the service. So if you are an unsuccessful candidate, but the service feels you should be given another chance, you may be invited to enlist to attend a prep school. Usually your enlistment is in the Reserves, not for active duty, so if after the ten-month course you still don't make an appointment as a cadet or a midshipman, you'll have to fulfill your Reserve commitment.

Selection to attend the prep school in no way guarantees an appointment to an academy. You must still follow the same procedure of obtaining a nomination and compete with all other service personnel. But the success of prep school graduates in gaining appointments is high enough to warrant taking the chance.

ROTC Scholarships

There are many scholarships available today based on your financial need. One that is based strictly on merit, without regard to your family or personal financial status, is the ROTC scholarship. These scholarships, which are available from the Air Force, Army, Marines, and Navy, help pay your way through school and lead to a commission as a second lieutenant or ensign at graduation.

As with any other scholarship, an ROTC scholarship is not easy to earn. Both the academic and physical requirements are high and the competition is stiff. But it's worth trying for because it will pay for your tuition, books, and fees, and also give you a tax-free allowance of $100 each month of the school year and about $100 a week during those four to six weeks you must attend training sessions each summer.

There are a lot of similarities among the programs of the various services. First of all, these scholarships are available to cover four, three, or two years in the Air Force and Army programs, and four or two years in the Navy/Marine programs. The four-year scholarships are awarded in worldwide competition among young men and women who are United States citizens and entering college for the first time. The three- and two-year scholarships are awarded competitively to students already enrolled in ROTC without a scholarship and to transfers from junior colleges who are eligible for advance ROTC placement.

The best part of all this is that if you win a scholarship you can go to the college or university of your choice, as long as they have an ROTC unit of the service from which you won the scholarship. This means that if you win an Army ROTC scholarship you can use it in over 280 colleges and universities. Air Force scholarship winners can use it in over 150 schools, Navy/Marine winners in 50.

As an ROTC student you'll lead essentially the same campus life as your non-ROTC classmates. You'll be on your own to make your arrangements for room and board; you can take whatever courses you want and need for your degree, and participate in any extracurricular activities as long as they don't interfere with your ROTC requirements.

Normally your ROTC classes and drills will take no more than five hours a week and the three summer training sessions will last no longer than six weeks each.

This all sounds pretty cushy, but as much as the military wants to train you to become an officer, it is still not a giveaway. If you win a scholarship you'll be required to enlist in that service's Reserves as an E-1. If you lose your scholarship for any reason that's beyond your control, you'll also be released from the Reserves, but if you decide to try to beat the system by goofing off or weaseling out of your contract commitment, you'll stand a good chance of being taken out of college and ordered from your Reserve status to active duty, where you'll start as an E-1 and could be held in for a period of up to four years.

If you complete the course you'll have to serve a minimum of six years after commissioning. Right now that six years is broken down to four years of active duty and two years in the Reserves, but it's subject to change.

Aside from the fact that your military subjects will be aimed at making you an officer in one particular service, the main difference between all the scholarship programs is in the academic areas your service wants you to major in while in school. Air Force ROTC scholarships are available to men and women who are willing to major in certain scientific, technical, mathematical, or engineering fields. The exception to this is men who desire to be pilots or navigators. They can major in just about anything provided they sign up for flying after graduation. The Army, like all large businesses, needs college graduates in a wide variety of fields, so its scholarship program is almost unrestricted when it comes to your choice of a major. The Navy leans toward technical training with the emphasis on engineering degrees, physics, mathematics, and chemistry. Those few students who are allowed to major in other fields are still expected to take some courses in calculus and physics.

The Marine scholarships come under what is called the Marine option of the Navy ROTC (NROTC) scholarship. You can take the NROTC scholarship exams and training with the intention of becoming a Marine second lieutenant instead of a Navy ensign. The Marines are also looking for technically or scientifically trained officers, but they have openings for other majors as well.

And all the services are looking for, and will bend over backward for, anyone who can qualify to become a pilot. They all offer some civilian pilot training to selected ROTC students still in college.

Non-Scholarship ROTC

You don't have to win a scholarship to study in one of the ROTC programs. For example, there are about 50,000 students registered in Army ROTC, but only about 6,500 of them are on scholarships.

The first two years of ROTC are open to almost any student who wants to take the course as an elective. If you want to give it a try, all you have to do is sign up for it at the same time and in the same way that you register for all your other courses.

All ROTC courses are for four years, but they are all divided into two segments of two years each. Unless you are on a scholarship, there is no military commitment for taking the first two years. But the final two years are only open to those selected by the ROTC officials, and the selection is usually highly competitive. Applicants must be able to meet all the academic and physical qualifications to become an officer. There is no scholarship assistance for those selected, but you will receive a tax-free allowance of $100 a month for each month of the school year for your final two years.

The non-scholarship program requires you to attend one summer training session, usually between your junior and senior year. This is about six weeks long and you'll be paid about $100 a week.

Students without ROTC training and at least two years of undergraduate or graduate work remaining may apply for the final two-year program, provided they successfully complete a catch-up-type basic camp the summer before entering the program.

The Air Force and the Army also have cross-enrollment agreements with hundreds of schools, including junior and community colleges. These agreements let you go to the school of your choice that doesn't have an ROTC unit, and commute to the nearest school hosting an ROTC unit for that training.

Your service obligation under the non-scholarship

program is also six years, but in this case it's from six months to two years of active duty and the rest in the Reserves.

ROTC Information

To find out the details about ROTC programs, both scholarship and non-scholarship, see your high-school counselor, any recruiter, or the commander of any ROTC unit. Or write to:

AFROTC Advisory Section
Maxwell AFB, Alabama 36112

Army ROTC
Fort Monroe, Virginia 23651

Commandant of the Marine Corps
Headquarters Marine Corps
Washington, D.C. 20380

NROTC
Navy Recruiting Command
4015 Wilson Blvd
Arlington, Virginia 22203

Other Commissioning Programs

We have spent a lot of time discussing the service academies and ROTC, because you can enter these programs leading to commissions right from high school. There is one other program you can enter as a college freshman. This is the Marine Platoon Leaders' Class (PLC).

The main difference between this and ROTC is that there are no classes during the school year. If you enter as a freshman or sophomore, you will attend two six-week PLC summer training sessions at the Officer Candidate School, Quantico, Virginia. If you enter PLC in your junior year you'll have one ten-week session. You may apply to receive financial assistance of $100 a month for up to three nine-month school years, or a total of $2700, but this adds to your active-duty obligation.

All the other programs leading to commissions require that you either already have your degree or be in your senior year.

The only one that offers you any financial assistance—and it could be substantial assistance—is the Navy's Nuclear Propulsion Officer Candidate Program, which provides more than $500 a month to qualified college seniors. You don't have to be studying nuclear physics or anything like it to qualify, but you must have taken math through integral calculus and one year of physics, and be willing to do a year of graduate study, at Navy expense, in nuclear-propulsion-plant theory and operation.

It might be appropriate to note that nuclear-trained officers are still in short supply, so the financial rewards are high. A bonus of up to $3000 is paid to all officers who successfully complete nuclear training, and if you sign up for another four years after your first hitch, you're eligible for a bonus as high as $20,000. In addition, you can earn a yearly incentive bonus of up to $4000 for each year you serve beyond your minimum requirement. That's long-term thinking, but if your career plans lie in that direction, it's nice to know.

If you think you might want to start your career as an officer but don't want to be bothered with it at all in school or during the summers, you can always apply to go to an officer-candidate program after graduation. All the services have them.

How to Put Your Best Foot Forward

When you're considering trying for an academy appointment or an ROTC scholarship, or following any other path to becoming an officer, it will pay you to start early and to try always to make a good impression at every step along the way. Remember, you'll be asking your government to invest anywhere from a few thousand dollars to up to $100,000 in your education. That's worth some time and effort.

The following are a few tips that should help you. (They are also valid in job hunting for a civilian job.)

1. Start early to gather the information you need. Your junior year isn't too soon.

2. Take a solid academic program in high school: four years of English and math, a heavy dose of the sciences, social sciences, and languages. Don't look for a snap program in high school and then expect to get what you want in college.

3. Participate in and try to excel in school extracurricular activities.

4. Stay in good physical condition.

5. Take part in sports. If you can't make the varsity, play intramurals.

6. Join JROTC, the Civil Air Patrol, the Sea Cadets, the scouts, or any other organization that will give you the

chance to learn leadership and test your leadership ability.

7. Take the required college-entrance tests (SAT or ACT) in your junior year. Then you can retake them in your senior year and perhaps improve your score.

8. Take the college-entrance tests as early as possible in your senior year to be certain you'll have the scores in time for each service's application deadline. And be sure to check the appropriate release blocks on the test sheet so that your score will be released to the service academy or scholarship committee as well as to the college of your choice.

9. Type or print legibly in ink all application forms and letters. The first impression you make is through your application, so don't fill it in with a stubby pencil. (Some students do, believe it or not.)

10. If you have to fill out forms, read and reread the directions to make sure you fill them out completely and correctly.

11. If a picture is required, take the time and the few dollars necessary to get a good color photo made of yourself, head and shoulders or full-length, whichever they request. And dress for the photo the same way you'd dress for an interview. A mere picture won't get you the appointment or scholarship, but it may help keep you in the running. If instead you send a beat-up snapshot or a group photo with a circle around you, all you're saying to the people handling your application is that you don't care enough about this to send the best. In that case they probably won't care about you either.

12. Don't be modest. In making out an application put down everything you did in or out of high school in the

way of services or activities. Don't just put down what you did in your senior year, but look back to when you were a lowly frosh, too. It's the total picture that counts. Every activity, every honor adds to your score.

13. If you held a part-time job that restricted your participation in sports or extracurricular activities, put that down. The number of hours you worked each week will probably score you points.

14. Be honest. They'll probably check.

15. If you need to add extra sheets, do so, but make sure your name or some other identification is on each sheet in case they become separated from the basic form.

16. If you're called for an interview, wear appropriate clothes. T-shirts and ragged jeans may make it with your friends, but they make the wrong impression for someone who professes a desire to become a military officer.

17. Try to relax at an interview. The board members or interviewers aren't there to bite your head off. In fact, they are probably rooting for you. They merely want to confirm the impression they have of you from your application. The way you impress them face to face can add significantly to your score. Don't be hesitant, but take enough time answering their questions to answer them well. Don't try to fool anyone with answers you don't believe but think they'd like to hear. If you don't believe in what you say, they'll know it. All the members on a board like this have been dealing with people for years, and they know how to spot, and downscore, a phony.

18. Before any interview, fill yourself in on current events and make sure you understand them. Since each applicant has a different background, one way interviewers and board members like to make everyone equal is to

ask questions about things outside school. Current events, including sports, is a favorite topic for this.

19. If something significant happens to you after you've submitted your application, be sure to send in a letter updating your file.

20. If you receive any kind of a message asking for additional information, send it promptly.

CHAPTER TEN

Afterwards: You're a Veteran

When you get out of the service, whether it's after a two-year tour, a six-year tour, or after twenty years of service, you'll pick up a new classification that brings with it a number of additional benefits. You'll be a veteran.

Benefits available from the Veterans Administration (VA) include: employment assistance, home loans, disability pensions, medical care, and low-cost life insurance.

At this point these benefits are a long way off for you, especially if you decide to make the military a career, but you should know about them so you can include them in your long-range plans.

Employment. As a veteran you will get preferential treatment from both federal and state employment offices. They will help you find a job and see that you get vocational counseling and testing. Being a veteran also automatically adds points to your test score for any U.S. civil service exam and for many state jobs.

You may also be entitled to state unemployment compensation while you job hunt after discharge.

Housing. The VA will help you get a loan to buy a house, mobile home, or condominium. It doesn't actually lend you the money, but guarantees repayment to any private lender who does lend you the money. One of the best features of a VA home loan is that it doesn't require a down payment, which in these days can amount to many thousands of dollars.

Disability Compensation. If anything happens to your health while you are in the service that handicaps your earning power after discharge, you will probably be entitled to monthly compensation payments from the VA for as long as you are disabled.

Medical Care. If you have a service-connected disability, you are eligible for free medical care. You may also be given care for non-service-connected problems if you can't pay for private medical care.

Life Insurance. When you leave the service your Servicemen's Group Life Insurance (SGLI) stops, but you can convert it to a low-cost Veterans' Group Life Insurance five-year-term policy. At the end of the five years you can convert that to a commercial whole-life policy, no matter what the condition of your health is at that time.

ONE FINAL BENEFIT—A LIFETIME INCOME

If after you have tried service life you decide you like it and want to make it a career, you are planting the seeds of a lifetime income.

There are few civilian retirement plans that can match the one offered by the military.

We have not dwelled on this, because the main idea of this book is that you should try the military before you decide, but you should also be aware of this major benefit that awaits you if you do stay in for at least twenty years. (There is a lot of discussion about changing the minimum to thirty years, but in early 1980 you could still retire after twenty years if you wanted to.)

If you retire after 20 years of service you should have attained a rank of at least E-7 as an enlisted person or 0-5 as an officer. Twenty-year retirement brings a lifetime income of 50 percent of your base pay at retirement time. It's impossible to predict what the base pay will be 20 years from now, but according to the pay scale in Appendix B, today an E-7 would receive $546 a month retirement pay and an 0-5 $1188. That's for life. And it also includes a twice-a-year automatic cost-of-living increase pegged to the consumer price index.

Twenty-year retirees are often young enough to start a profitable second career and still draw retirement pay on top of their civilian salary.

If you stay in the service longer than 20 years, you will get an increase of 2.5 percent of your base pay for every year you were in; for example, 52.5 percent for 21 years, 62.5 percent for 25 years, up to a maximum of 75 percent for thirty years of service. A 30-year enlisted person should have made the top enlisted grade and therefore would retire at $1222 a month at current pay scales, and an officer should have made 0-6 and would retire at over $2260 a month.

In addition, retired personnel continue to be able to use many of the fringe benefits of active-duty personnel, such as the commissary and exchanges and financial assistance in paying medical bills.

Added to all the other benefits, this final one makes a military career worth even more consideration.

Appendix A

TABLE OF COMPARATIVE RANKS

Pay Grade	Air Force	Army	Marine	Navy/Coast Guard
E-1	Airman Basic	Recruit	Private	Seaman Recruit
E-2	Airman	Private	Private First Class	Seaman Apprentice
E-3	Airman First Class	Private First Class	Lance Corporal	Seaman
E-4	Senior Airman or Sergeant	Corporal or Specialist 4	Corporal	Petty Officer Third Class
E-5	Staff Sergeant	Sergeant or Specialist 5	Sergeant	Petty Officer Second Class
E-6	Technical Sergeant	Staff Sergeant or Specialist 6	Staff Sergeant	Petty Officer First Class
E-7	Master Sergeant	Sergeant First Class or Platoon Sergeant or Specialist 7	Gunnery Sergeant	Chief Petty Officer
E-8	Senior Master Sergeant	Master Sergeant or First Sergeant	Master Sergeant or Officer	Senior Chief Petty Officer
E-9	Chief Master Sergeant	Sergeant Major	Master Gunnery Sergeant or Sergeant Major	Master Chief Petty Officer
W-1	Warrant Officer			
W-2	Chief Warrant Officer			
W-3				
W-4				

Pay Grade	Air Force/Army/Marines	Navy/Coast Guard
O-1	Second Lieutenant	Ensign
O-2	First Lieutenant	Lieutenant Junior Grade
O-3	Captain	Lieutenant
O-4	Major	Lieutenant Commander
O-5	Lieutenant Colonel	Commander
O-6	Colonel	Captain
O-7	Brigadier General	Commodore
O-8	Major General	Rear Admiral
O-9	Lieutenant General	Vice Admiral
O-10	General (4 star) General of the Army or General of the Air Force (5 star)	Admiral (4 star) Fleet Admiral (5 star)

Appendix B

PAY AND ALLOWANCE RATES
Basic Pay Rates

PAY GRADE	Years Under 2	2	3	4	6	8	10
COMMISSIONED OFFICERS							
O-10	—	—	—	—	—	—	—
O-9	—	—	—	—	—	—	—
O-8	—	—	—	—	—	—	—
O-7	—	—	—	—	—	—	—
O-6	—	—	—	—	—	—	—
O-5	1395.90	1639.20	1752.30	—	—	—	1805.70
O-4	1176.60	1432.20	1528.20	—	1556.10	1625.40	1736.10
O-3	1093.50	1222.20	1306.50	1445.70	1514.70	1569.60	1653.90
O-2	953.10	1041.30	1250.70	1293.00	1319.70	—	—
O-1	827.40	861.30	1041.30	—	—	—	—
COMMISSIONED OFFICERS WITH OVER 4 YEARS SERVICE AS ENLISTED MEMBERS							
O-3	—	—	—	1445.70	1514.70	1569.60	1653.90
O-2	—	—	—	1293.00	1319.70	1361.70	1432.20
O-1	—	—	—	1041.30	1112.10	1153.20	1194.90
WARRANT OFFICERS							
W-4	—	—	—	1222.20	1278.00	1334.40	1390.20
W-3	—	—	—	1112.10	1125.30	1207.50	1278.00
W-2	—	959.10	—	987.70	1041.30	1098.30	1139.70
W-1	738.90	847.20	—	917.70	959.10	1000.50	1041.30
ENLISTED MEMBERS							
E-9	—	—	—	—	—	—	1265.40
E-8	—	—	—	—	—	1061.70	1091.40
E-7	—	—	829.80	858.60	888.30	916.20	945.60
E-6	—	—	727.20	757.80	786.00	814.80	844.80
E-5	—	611.70	641.40	669.30	713.10	742.20	771.90
E-4	540.30	570.60	603.90	651.00	676.80	—	—
E-3	519.60	548.10	570.30	592.80	—	—	—
E-2	500.10	—	—	—	—	—	—
E-1	448.80	—	—	—	—	—	—

12	14	16	18	20	22	26
—	—	—	—	—	—	4961.10
—	—	—	—	—	4084.80	4377.00
—	—	—	—	—	3946.20	—
—	—	—	3431.10	—	—	—
—	—	2446.50	2571.60	2627.10	2779.80	3014.70
1902.30	2029.50	2181.60	2307.00	2376.60	2459.70	—
1833.90	1917.60	2001.30	2057.10	—	—	—
1736.10	1778.70	—	—	—	—	—
—	—	—	—	—	—	—
—	—	—	—	—	—	—
1736.10	1805.70	—	—	—	—	—
1487.40	1528.20	—	—	—	—	—
1236.60	1293.00	—	—	—	—	—
1487.40	1556.10	1611.30	1653.90	1707.90	1765.20	1902.30
1319.70	1361.70	1402.50	1445.70	1501.50	1556.10	1611.30
1181.40	1222.20	1265.10	1306.50	1347.90	1402.50	—
1084.20	1125.30	1166.70	1207.50	1250.70	—	—
1294.20	1323.60	1354.20	1384.20	1411.20	1485.60	1629.60
1120.50	1149.90	1179.90	1207.20	1236.90	1309.50	1455.60
975.00	1019.10	1047.90	1077.60	1091.40	1164.90	1309.50
883.30	916.20	945.60	960.00	—	—	—
800.10	814.80	—	—	—	—	—
—	—	—	—	—	—	—
—	—	—	—	—	—	—
—	—	—	—	—	—	—

Note: Military pay is reviewed by Congress each year. Pay raises are usually approved as of October 1. This is the pay scale as of October 1, 1979.

Subsistence Allowance

Officers: ....67.21 per month

Enlisted Members:

When on leave
or authorized
to mess separately: ....3.21 per day

When rations in-kind
are not available: ....3.62 per day

When assigned to duty
under emergency
conditions where
no messing facilities
of the United States
are available: ....4.79 per day

Quarters Allowance

Pay Grade	Without Kin Full Rate	Without Kin Partial Rate	With Kin
O-10	383.10	50.70	479.10
O-9	383.10	50.70	479.10
O-8	383.10	50.70	479.10
O-7	383.10	50.70	479.10
O-6	343.80	39.60	419.40
O-5	316.80	33.00	381.60
O-4	282.30	26.70	340.50
O-3	248.10	22.20	306.30
O-2	215.40	17.70	272.70
O-1	168.00	13.20	219.00
W-4	271.80	25.20	328.20
W-3	242.40	20.70	298.80
W-2	210.90	15.90	268.20
W-1	190.50	13.80	246.60
E-9	205.20	18.60	288.60
E-8	189.00	15.30	266.70
E-7	160.80	12.00	248.10
E-6	146.10	9.90	228.30
E-5	140.40	8.70	209.70
E-4	123.90	8.10	184.50
E-3	110.70	7.80	160.80
E-2	97.80	7.20	160.80
E-1	92.40	6.90	160.80

Index